Racine and Shakespeare

Stendhal

ALMA CLASSICS

Stendhal

RACINE AND SHAKESPEARE

Translated by Guy Daniels

ALMA CLASSICS
an imprint of

ALMA BOOKS LTD
3 Castle Yard
Richmond
Surrey TW10 6TF
United Kingdom
www.almaclassics.com

Racine and Shakespeare first published by the Crowell-Collier Press
Company in 1962
A new edition first published by Alma Classics in 2011
This new edition first published by Alma Classics in 2019

Translation © Guy Daniels, 1962

Cover design: Will Dady

Printed and bound by CPI Group (UK) Ltd, Croydon, CR0 4YY

ISBN: 978-1-84749-849-6

Contents

RACINE AND SHAKESPEARE

ON MOLIÈRE, REGNARD, AND OTHER MATTERS

RACINE AND SHAKESPEARE II

1823

RACINE AND SHAKESPEARE

Intelligenti pauca

Preface

NOTHING RESEMBLES less than we do those *marquis* in embroidered coats and big black periwigs costing a thousand *écus* who, about 1670, judged the plays of Racine and Molière.

Those two great men aimed at flattering the taste of the *marquis* and worked for them.

It is my contention that henceforth tragedies should be written for us, the young people of the year of grace 1823, who are argumentative, serious, and a bit envious. Those tragedies should be in prose. In our day, the alexandrine line is often nothing more than a means of concealing stupidity.

The reigns of Charles VI, Charles VII, and the noble Francis I should be for us a rich source of tragedies on national themes, of deep and lasting interest. But how can one depict with any degree of truth the bloody catastrophes recounted by Philippe de Comines, or the scandalous chronicle of Jean de Troyes, if it is absolutely impossible to use the word *pistolet* in a line of tragic poetry?

Dramatic poetry in France is in the stage at which the famous David found the art of painting about 1780. The first attempts of this bold genius were in the aerial and vapid style of the Lagrenées, the Fragonards, and the Vanloos. He painted three or four pictures that were very much acclaimed. Finally—and it is this which will make him immortal—he realized that the insipid style of the old French school no longer suited the severe taste of a people in whom a craving for vigorous deeds was beginning to develop. M. David taught painters to quit following in the steps of the Lebruns and the Mignards and have the courage to portray Brutus and the Horatii. If we had continued to follow the ways of the century of Louis XIV, we would never have been anything more than feeble imitators.

Everything indicates that we are on the eve of a similar revolution in poetry. Until the day of success arrives, we defenders of the *romantic genre* will have abuse heaped upon us. But finally that great day will arrive, and French youth will awaken. They will be astounded, those noble young people, to think that for such a long time, and with so much seriousness, they had applauded such utterly foolish things.

The two articles that follow—written in only a few hours and with more zeal than talent, as you will notice only too soon—were published in Numbers 9 and 12 of the *Paris Monthly Review*.

The author, who, professionally, is far removed from any literary pretensions, has said without art or eloquence what seems to him the truth.

He has been engaged throughout his life in other kinds of work, and he is in no way entitled to discuss literature. If in spite of himself, his ideas at times assume a trenchant aspect, it is because, out of respect for the public, he wanted to state them clearly and in a few words.

If, paying heed only to a well-founded mistrust of his ability, the author had surrounded his remarks with an unassailable array of those dubitative and elegant forms befitting anyone so unfortunate as not to admire everything admired by those who control public opinion, no doubt the interests of his modesty would have been completely sheltered. But in this case he would have gone on at much greater length. And in these times in which we are living, one has to do things in a hurry—especially when it is a question of literary bagatelles.

Chapter 1

In order to write tragedies which will interest the public of 1823, should one follow the procedures of Racine or those of Shakespeare?

THIS QUESTION seems to have worn itself out in France; and yet we have heard the arguments of one side only. The newspapers that are the most opposed in their political opinions, both the *Quotidienne* and the *Constitutionnel*, agree on only one thing: they proclaim that French drama is not only the best drama in the world, but the only rational drama. If that poor thing, Romanticism, had a claim it wanted to publicize, all newspapers of all shades of opinion would be equally closed to it.

But this apparent disfavor in no way frightens us, because it is a matter of partisanship. We reply to this with a single fact.

What literary work has enjoyed the greatest success in France in the last ten years?

The novels of Sir Walter Scott.

What are the novels of Sir Walter Scott?

Romantic tragedy, intertwined with long descriptions.

By way of objection, our opponents will cite the success of *Les Vêpres siciliennes, Le Paria, Les Machabées,* and *Régulus.*

These plays provide a good deal of pleasure; but they do not provide a *dramatic pleasure.* The public—which, incidentally, does not enjoy any extreme freedom—likes to hear generous sentiments expressed in beautiful lines of poetry.

But this pleasure is of an *epic* nature, not a dramatic one. There is never that degree of illusion necessary for a profound emotion. It is for this reason—one of which the young public itself is unaware (because at the age of twenty, whatever is said to the contrary, one wants to enjoy things, not

11

reason about them; and this is quite right)—it is for this secret reason that the young public of the second French theatre[1] puts so few demands upon the plot element in the plays that it applauds with the greatest transports. What, for example, is more ridiculous than the plot of *Le Paria?* It does not stand up to the least bit of analysis. Everybody has made this criticism; and yet this criticism has not had any effect. Why? Because the public wants only beautiful poetry. The public goes to the contemporary French theatre expecting to hear a series of very pompous odes which, incidentally, express forcefully some generous sentiments. If they are introduced by a few transitional lines of poetry, that suffices. It is like the ballets of the Rue Pelletier: the action must be gone through for the sole purpose of introducing some beautiful steps and in order to justify, after a fashion, some pleasant dances.

I address myself fearlessly to those misguided young people who believed they were being patriotic and defending the national honor when they hissed Shakespeare because he was English. Since I am full of esteem for hard-working young people, the hope of France, I shall talk to them in the severe language of truth.

The entire dispute between Racine and Shakespeare comes down to whether, while observing the two unities of *time* and *place,* one can write plays that vitally interest nineteenth-century audiences—plays that make them weep and shudder or, in other words, that give them *dramatic* pleasures rather than the *epic* pleasures that make us rush to the fiftieth performance of *Le Paria* or *Régulus.*

I maintain that adherence to the two unities of *time* and *place* is a French habit; a habit with very deep roots; a habit from which we shall free ourselves only with difficulty, because Paris is the salon of Europe and sets the fashion for Europe. But I also maintain that these unities are by no means necessary for producing profound emotion and the genuine dramatic effect.

[1] Le Théâtre de l'Odéon. [Translator's note.]

Why, I will ask the partisans of *Classicism*, do you demand that the action depicted in a tragedy cover not more than twenty-four or thirty-six hours? And that the setting represented on the stage not change—or at any rate, as Voltaire says, that the changes of setting not extend beyond the different rooms of a palace?

THE ACADEMICIAN: Because it is not credible that an action represented in two hours should encompass a week or a month; or that in a few moments the actors should go from Venice to Cyprus, as in Shakespeare's *Othello*, or from Scotland to the English court, as in *Macbeth*.

THE ROMANTIC: Not only is that incredible and impossible; but it is likewise impossible that the action encompass twenty-four or thirty-six hours.[2]

THE ACADEMICIAN: Heaven forbid that we should be so absurd as to claim that the fictitious duration of the action should correspond exactly to the *material* time consumed by the performance. If this were the case, the rules would be actual fetters on genius. In the imitative arts, one must be strict but not rigorous. The spectator can easily imagine that several hours have passed during the interval of the intermissions—all the more so because he is diverted by the symphonies played by the orchestra.

THE ROMANTIC: Be careful of what you say, Monsieur. You are giving me a great advantage. You agree, then, that the spectator can *imagine* that more time is passing than that during which he is seated in the theatre. But tell me: Can he imagine a time passing that is double the real time, triple, quadruple, or a hundred times greater? Where shall we stop?

THE ACADEMICIAN: You are odd, you modern philosophers. You blame poetics because, so you say, it fetters genius. And now you want us to apply the rule of the *unity of time* with all the rigor and exactitude of mathematics, in order for it to be plausible. Is it not enough for you that it obviously contravenes all credibility for the spectator to imagine that a year, a month, or even a week has passed since he got his ticket and entered the theatre?

[2] Dialogue of Ermeo Visconti in *Il Conciliatore*, Milan, 1818.

THE ROMANTIC: And who told you that the spectator cannot imagine that?

THE ACADEMICIAN: It is reason that tells me.

THE ROMANTIC: I beg your pardon. Reason cannot possibly teach you this. How could you know that the spectator can imagine that twenty-four hours have passed, whereas actually he has only been sitting in his box for two hours, unless experience had taught you this? How could you know that those hours that seem so long to a man who is bored, seem to fly when a person is being amused, unless experience had told you. In a word, it is *experience* alone that must settle the issue between you and me.

THE ACADEMICIAN: Yes, no doubt it is experience.

THE ROMANTIC: Well, experience has already spoken against you. In England, for two centuries now, and in Germany, during the past fifty years, they have been performing tragedies whose action covers entire months; and the spectators' imagination accomodates itself perfectly to this.

THE ACADEMICIAN: But now you are giving me the example of foreigners—and Germans at that!

THE ROMANTIC: Some other time we shall discuss this unquestionable superiority of the Frenchman in general, and the inhabitant of Paris in particular, over all the other peoples of the world. I shall be fair: this superiority is a *matter of feeling* with you. You are despots spoiled by two centuries of flattery. Fate willed that you Parisians should become responsible for making literary reputations in Europe. A woman of wit, known for her *enthusiasm* for the beauties of nature, once exclaimed, in order to please the Parisians: "The most beautiful stream in the world is the stream of the Rue du Bac!" All the genteel writers—not only in France but throughout Europe—have flattered you in order to obtain a bit of literary fame in return. And what you call *inner feeling* and *moral evidence* is nothing more than the moral evidence of a spoiled child; in other words, the habit of being flattered.

But let us get back to the point. Can you deny that the inhabitant of London or Edinburgh, the compatriots of Fox and Sheridan, who are perhaps not utter fools, see performances of tragedies like *Macbeth*, for example, without being shocked in the slightest? Now this play, which every year is applauded an infinite number of times in England and America, begins with the assassination of the king and the flight of his sons. And it ends with the return of these same princes at the head of an army that they have assembled in England in order to dethrone the bloody Macbeth. This series of actions necessarily requires several months.

THE ACADEMICIAN: Ah! You will never persuade me that the English and the Germans, even if they are foreigners, really imagine that entire months pass while they are at the theatre.

THE ROMANTIC: Just as you will never persuade me that the French spectators believe that twenty-four hours pass while they are watching a performance of *Iphigénie en Aulide*.

THE ACADEMICIAN (*impatient*): What a difference!

THE ROMANTIC: Let us not become incensed. And please observe carefully what is going on in your head. Try to draw aside for a moment the veil that habit has thrown over acts which take place so rapidly that you have lost the ability to follow them with your eye and see them *occur*. Let us come to an agreement on the word *illusion*. When one says that the spectator imagines that the time necessary for the events represented on the stage has passed, one does not mean that the spectator's illusion extends to the point of believing that all this time has really elapsed. The fact is that the spectator, caught up and carried along by the story, is not shocked by anything. He gives no thought whatsoever to the time that has passed. Your Parisian spectator sees Agamemnon awaken Arcas at exactly seven o'clock. He witnesses the arrival of Iphigenia; and he sees her led to the altar where the Jesuitic Calchas is waiting for her. If anyone asked him, he would of course reply that these events required several hours. And yet, if during the quarrel between Achilles and Agamemnon he were to take out his watch, it would show the hour of 8:15. What spectator would be surprised by this? Nonetheless, the play that he is applauding has already lasted for several hours.

The truth of the matter is that even your Parisian spectator is accustomed to seeing time move at different rates on the stage and in the other part of the theatre. This is a fact that you cannot deny. It is clear that even in Paris, even at the Théâtre-Français in the Rue de Richelieu, the spectator's imagination lends itself easily to the poet's suppositions. The spectator, quite naturally, pays no attention to the intervals of time required by the poet; just as in sculpture he does not take it into his head to reproach Dupaty or Bosio for the fact that their figures lack movement. This is one of the infirmities of art. The spectator, when he is not a pedant, is concerned only with the acts and developments of passions that are presented to his view. Precisely the same thing happens in the head of the Parisian who applauds *Iphigénie en Aulide* and in that of the Scotsman who admires the story of his former kings, Macbeth and Duncan. The only difference is that the Parisian, being a child of good family, has acquired the habit of mocking others.

THE ACADEMICIAN: In other words, according to you the theatrical illusion is the same for both?

THE ROMANTIC: To have illusions, to be in a state of *illusion,* means to deceive oneself, according to the *Dictionary* of the Academy. An *illusion,* M. Guizot says, is the effect of a thing or an idea that deceives us by its misleading appearance. Illusion therefore means the act of a man who believes a thing that does not exist—as in dreams, for example. Theatrical illusion would be the act of a man who believes that the things that take place on the stage really exist.

Last year (August 1822) a soldier who was standing guard in the theatre in Baltimore, upon seeing Othello, in the fifth act of the tragedy of that name, about to kill Desdemona, cried out: "It will never be said that in my presence a damned nigger killed a white woman." At the same moment the soldier shot at the actor who was playing Othello and broke his arm. Not one year passes but what the newspapers report similar incidents.

Now that soldier was entertaining an *illusion:* he believed in the reality of what was happening on the stage. But an ordinary spectator at the moment when his pleasure is most intense—at the moment when he is enthusiastically *applaud-*

ing Talma-Manlius[3] saying to his friend, "Do you recognize this writing?"—by virtue of the very fact that he applauds, does not have a *complete illusion,* because he is applauding Talma and not the Roman, Manlius. Manlius does nothing deserving of applause. His act is very simple and entirely in his own interest.

THE ACADEMICIAN: I beg your pardon, my friend, but what you have just said is a commonplace.

THE ROMANTIC: I beg your pardon, my friend, but what you have just said represents the defeat of a man made incapable of close reasoning by an ingrained habit of indulging in elegant phrases.

It is impossible for you not to agree that the illusion one seeks at the theatre is not a complete illusion. *Complete* illusion is the kind experienced by the soldier standing guard in the theatre in Baltimore. It is impossible for you not to agree that the spectators know very well that they are in a theatre and watching a work of art, not a real event.

THE ACADEMICIAN: Who would think of denying that?

THE ROMANTIC: Then you grant that there is *imperfect illusion?* You had better be on your guard.

Do you believe that from time to time—for example, two or three times in one act, and for only a second or two each time—the illusion is complete?

THE ACADEMICIAN: That is by no means clear. In order to give you an answer, I should have to go back to the theatre several times and observe my actions.

THE ROMANTIC: Ah! That is a charming reply, and one full of good faith. One can easily see that you belong to the Academy and that you no longer need the votes of your colleagues to be admitted. A man who had yet to make his reputation as a learned *littérateur* would take pains to avoid being so clear and reasoning in a manner so precise. You had better be on your guard: if you continue to be of good faith, we shall agree with each other.

It seems to me that these moments of *complete illusion* are

[3] I.e., François-Joseph Talma, the famous tragic actor, in the leading role of *Manlius Capitolinus,* by Lafosse d'Aubigny, a playwright of the eighteenth century. [Translator's note.]

more frequent than is generally supposed, especially than is admitted in literary discussions, as a matter of fact. But these moments are of infinitely brief duration—for example, a half-second or a quarter-second. One very quickly forgets Manlius and sees only Talma. Such moments last longer with young women, and that is why they cry so copiously at a tragedy.

But let us try to discover at what moments in a tragedy the spectator can hope to find these delicious instants of *complete illusion*.

Such charming instants do not occur when there is a change of scene; nor at the precise moment when the poet requires the spectator to skip over twelve or fifteen days; nor when the poet is obliged to give a long speech to one of his characters for the sole purpose of informing the spectator of a previous fact about which he must know; nor, again, when there are three or four lines which are admirable and remarkable *as poetry*.

These delicious and very rare instants of *complete illusion* are encountered only in the warmth of a lively scene when there is a rapid exchange of lines among the actors. For example, when Hermione says to Orestes, who has just assassinated Pyrrhus by her order:

Who told you?

One will never encounter these moments of *complete illusion* at the instant when a murder is committed on the stage or when the guards come to arrest a character and take him to prison. We cannot believe any of these things to be real, and they never produce an illusion. These bits are written only to introduce the scenes in which the spectators experience those half-seconds that are so delicious. *Now I maintain that these brief moments of complete illusion are found more often in the tragedies of Shakespeare than in the tragedies of Racine.*

All the pleasure one derives from the tragic spectacle depends upon the frequency of these brief moments of illusion *and upon the state of emotion in which the spectator is left during the intervals between them.*

One of the things most opposed to the birth of these moments of illusion is admiration—however well-founded it may be—for the beautiful poetic lines of a tragedy.

It is much worse if one decides he wants to judge the *poetic lines* of a tragedy. But this is precisely the state of soul of the Parisian spectator when he first goes to see that much-lauded tragedy *Le Paria*.

Here we have the question of *romanticism* reduced to its ultimate terms. If you are of bad faith, or if you lack sensitivity, or if you have been petrified by Laharpe, you will deny me my brief moments of perfect illusion.

And I admit that there is nothing I can say in reply to you. Your feelings are not something material that I can extract from your own heart and hold up in front of your eyes to confound you.

I say to you: You should have such and such a feeling at this moment. All men who are generally well organized experience such a feeling at this moment. And you will reply: Please pardon my use of the expression, *but that is not true*.

As for me, I have nothing further to add. I have arrived at the last confines of what logic can grasp in poetry.

THE ACADEMICIAN: Your metaphysics is abominably obscure. Do you hope, with that, to make people hiss Racine?

THE ROMANTIC: First of all, only charlatans claim that they can teach algebra or extract a tooth without some pain. The question we are discussing is one of the most difficult that the human mind can undertake.

As for Racine, I am pleased that you mentioned that great man. His name has been made an insult for us; but his glory is immortal. He will always be one of the greatest geniuses to stir the astonishment and admiration of men. Is Caesar less a great general because gunpowder has been invented since his campaigns against our ancestors, the Gauls? All we claim is that if Caesar were to return to the world, his first concern would be to have cannons in his army. Would anyone say that Catinat or Luxembourg were greater generals than Caesar because they possessed a park of artillery, and because in three days they captured places that would have withstood the Roman legions for a month? It would have been a fine bit of reasoning if someone had said to Francis I at Marignan: "You must not use your artillery. Caesar had no cannons. Do you think you are more clever than Caesar?"

If persons of unquestionable talent like MM. Chénier, Lemercier, and Delavigne had dared to free themselves from rules whose absurdity has been recognized since Racine, they would have given us better plays than *Tibère, Agamemnon,* or *Les Vêpres siciliennes.* Is not *Pinto* a hundred times better than *Clovis, Orovèse, Cyrus,* or any other very correct tragedy of M. Lemercier?

Racine did not believe that tragedies could be written any other way. If he lived in our time and dared to follow the new rules, he would do a hundred times better than *Iphigénie.* Instead of arousing only admiration, a rather cold sentiment, he would cause torrents of tears to flow. Is there any man, of even a modicum of education, who does not derive more pleasure from seeing M. Lebrun's *Marie Stuart* at the Théâtre-Français than Racine's *Bajazet?* And yet M. Lebrun's lines of poetry are very weak. The great difference in the degree of pleasure is due to the fact that M. Lebrun has dared to be quasi-romantic.

THE ACADEMICIAN: You have talked a long time. You have perhaps spoken well, but you have not convinced me.

THE ROMANTIC: I was expecting that. But then, too, this rather lengthy intermission is going to end. The curtain is going up. I merely wanted to relieve the boredom by making you a bit angry. You must agree that I have succeeded.

This marks the end of the dialogue between the two adversaries—a dialogue that I actually heard in the pit of the theatre on the Rue Chantereine, and whose participants I could name if I wished.[4] The Romantic was polite and did not want to annoy the amiable Academician, who was much older than he. Otherwise he would have added: In order to be able still to read what is in one's own heart; in order that the veil of habit may be torn away; in order to be able to put oneself in a receptive state for the moments of *complete illu-*

4 Much of the dialogue was in fact adopted from Ermeo Visconti. [Translator's note.]

sion that we are discussing, one must have a soul susceptible to lively impressions; one must not be more than forty years old.

We are creatures of habit. If those habits are subjected to shock, we shall for a long time be aware only of the annoyances thrust upon us. Let us suppose that Talma comes on stage and plays Manlius with his hair powdered and arranged *en ailes de pigeon*. We would do nothing but laugh throughout the performance. Would it really be less sublime? No; but we would not see its sublime quality. Now Lekain would have produced *exactly the same effect in 1760* if he had come on stage *without* powdered hair to play this same role of Manlius. During the entire performance the audience would have been aware only of their *shocked habit*. This is precisely our situation in France with regard to Shakespeare. He disturbs a great many of those ridiculous habits that we have contracted from the assiduous reading of Laharpe and the other little perfumed rhetoricians of the eighteenth century. And what is worse, we have the vanity to maintain that these bad habits are rooted in nature.

The young people are still capable of recovering from this error of *amour-propre*. Since their souls are susceptible to lively impressions, pleasure can make them forget their vanity. But this cannot be demanded of a man older than forty. People of this age in Paris have taken their position on all things—even on things much more important than knowing whether, in order to write interesting tragedies in 1823, one should follow the system of Racine or that of Shakespeare.

Chapter 2

Laughter

What will you do, Monsieur, with the nose of a churchwarden?

REGNARD

A GERMAN PRINCE known for his love of literature has recently offered a prize for the best philosophical dissertation on laughter. I hope that this prize will be won by a Frenchman. Wouldn't it be ridiculous if we were beaten in this competition? It seems to me that more jokes are made during one evening in Paris than in the whole of Germany during a month.

Nonetheless, this program on the subject of laughter has been drawn up in German. What we have to do is to understand its nature and its nuances. We have to reply clearly and concisely to that difficult question: *What is laughter?*

The great misfortune is that the judges are Germans. It is to be feared that a few pseudo thoughts, elegantly disseminated through twenty pages of academic phrases and learnedly cadenced periodic sentences, will strike these crude judges as only so much nothingness. This is a warning that I feel I must give to those young writers who are at once simple and so affected, natural and so mannered, eloquent but with so few ideas:

La gloire du distique et l'espoir du quatrain.

(The glory of the couplet and the hope of the quatrain.)

In this case it is necessary to find some ideas—something assuredly very impertinent. Those Germans are so barbarous!

What is laughter? Hobbes replies: *This physical convulsion, familiar to everyone, is produced by the unexpected sight of our superiority over someone else.*

Look at that young man passing by who has dressed himself up with such great care. He is walking on tiptoe. In the

22

glad expression on his face, one can discern both self-satisfaction and the certitude of success. He is going to a ball. Now he is already under the porte-cochère, in a clutter of lampions and lackeys. He is rushing toward pleasure. But he takes a fall, and when he gets up he is covered with mud from head to toe. His erstwhile white waistcoat, so skillfully tailored, and his tie, so elegantly knotted—all is covered with stinking black mud. From the carriages behind his own comes a general burst of laughter. The porter at the door holds his sides; the crowd of lackeys, laughing to the point of tears, form a circle around the unfortunate young man.

Comedy must be presented with clarity. Our superiority over someone else must be clearly seen.

But this superiority is something so trivial, and so easily destroyed by the least reflection, that we must see it unexpectedly.

Hence these two requirements for the comic: clarity and unexpected occurrence.

If the disadvantage of the person we are supposed to laugh at reminds us right away that we, too, might encounter that misfortune, there is no laughter.

If the handsome young man on his way to the ball is sly enough, after falling in the mud and getting up again, to limp and give the impression that he has been badly hurt, the laughter stops in a trice and gives way to fear.

The reason for this is very simple: there is no more enjoyment of our superiority. On the contrary, there is the spectacle of misfortune for us: I, too, in getting out of my carriage, might break my leg.

People have been making jokes in France for two hundred years, now. Hence a joke must be very clever; otherwise it is understood from the very beginning, and the element of the unexpected is lost.

One other thing. It is essential that I accord a certain degree of esteem to the person at whom I am supposed to laugh. I value very highly the talent of M. Picard. In some of his comedies, however, the characters intended to amuse us have such low morals that I do not admit any comparison between them and myself. As soon as they have spoken four lines,

I hold them in utter contempt. There is nothing more of a ridiculous nature that I can, or need to, learn about these people.

A printer in Paris wrote a religious tragedy entitled *Joshua*. He printed it with the greatest possible luxury and sent it to his famous colleague, Bodoni, at Parma. Some time later the author-printer took a trip to Italy and went to see his friend Bodoni. "What do you think of my tragedy, *Joshua?*" "Ah, what beautiful things in it!" "Then you think the work will bring me some fame?" "Ah, my dear friend, it will make you immortal." "And the characters—what do you think of them?" "Sublime and perfectly sustained—especially the capital letters."

Bodoni, a devotee of his art, saw only the *typographical characters* in his friend's tragedy. This story made me laugh much more than it deserves. That was because I knew the author of *Joshua* and have the *very highest regard for him*. He is a sensible man with good manners and even intelligence, well endowed with talents for the book trade. All in all, the only fault I see in him is a bit of vanity—the same trait at which Bodoni's naïve reply made me laugh.

The *unrestrained laughter* provoked in us by Shakespeare's Falstaff when, in his account to Prince Henry (who later became the famous King Henry V), he gets started on the story of the twenty rogues who grew out of four rogues dressed in buckram—this laughter is delicious only because Falstaff is a most merry and infinitely witty man. By contrast, we hardly even laugh at the stupidities of Father Cassander.[1] Our superiority over him is a thing too well known in advance.

The laughter provoked in us by a fool like M. Maclou de Beaubuisson (of *Le Comédien d'Etampes*) contains an element of vengeance for boredom.

I have noticed that in society, when a pretty woman says of another woman who is dancing, "Good Heavens, how ridiculous she is!" it is almost always said with an air of

[1] "Pantaloon"; a stock character in popular French and Italian comedy: a foolish old man inevitably the butt of the clown's jokes. [Translator's note.]

malice rather than one of gaiety. Translate "ridiculous" by "odious."

After having laughed like a fool tonight at M. Maclou de Beaubuisson, very well acted by Bernard-Léon, it occurred to me that I had realized, perhaps vaguely, that this ridiculous person had been able to arouse feelings of love in pretty women of the provinces—women who but for their lack of taste could have been completely captivating to me. The laughter of a very handsome young man who had many successes with women migh not have had the nuance of vengeance that I thought I noticed in my own laughter.

Since ridicule is a great punishment among the French, they often laugh out of vengeance. This particular laughter is irrelevant to our discussion and should not enter into our analysis. It was merely necessary to take note of it in passing. Any laughter that is *affected* is, by that token alone, devoid of significance. It is like Father Morellet's opinion in favor of tithing and the priory of Thimer.

Everyone knows five or six excellent stories that circulate in society: one always laughs at *disappointed vanity*. If the story is told in a prolix manner—if the raconteur uses too many words and takes time to describe too many details—the listener surmises the end of the story, toward which he is being led too slowly. There is no laughter because there is no more surprise.

If, on the contrary, the raconteur skips over parts of his story and rushes toward the denouement, there is no laughter because the story lacks the extreme clarity it requires. Notice that very often the storyteller repeats twice the five or six words that make up the denouement of his story. If he knows what he is doing—if he has the charming art of being neither obscure nor too clear—the harvest of laughter is much greater at the second repetition than at the first.

The absurd, when carried to the extreme, often provokes laughter and provides a lively and delicious kind of merriment. This is the secret of Voltaire in the diatribe of Doctor Akakia and in his other pamphlets. Doctor Akakia (viz., Maupertuis) himself utters the absurdities that a shrewd fellow might employ to make light of his systems. On this point, I am well aware that I should offer some quotations;

but I don't have a single French book in my retreat at Montmorency. I trust that my readers, if I have any, will be able to remember this charming volume of their edition of Voltaire, entitled *Facéties*, very pleasing imitations of which I often encounter in the *Miroir*.

In his plays, Voltaire employed this practice of putting into the mouths of the comic characters themselves a lively and brilliant description of the ridiculous ideas that obsessed them; and that great man must have been very surprised to see that no one laughed. This was because it is too much against nature for a man to mock himself so clearly. When, in social gatherings, we deliberately make ourselves ridiculous, it is still done out of an excess of vanity. We are stealing this pleasure from the malice of people whose envy we have excited.

But to fabricate a character like Fier-en-Fat is not to portray the foibles of the human heart. It is simply to have the burlesque phrases of a pamphlet uttered in the first person, and to give them life.

Is it not remarkable that Voltaire, who was so amusing in satire and in the philosophical novel, was never able to write a comic scene that made people laugh? Carmontelle, on the contrary, does not have a single skit in which this talent is not found. He had too much of a natural quality, as did Sedaine. They lacked the wit of Voltaire, who in this genre had only wit.

The foreign critics have observed that there is always an element of malice in the most amusing jokes of *Candide* and *Zadig*. Voltaire, himself richly endowed, took pleasure in parading before our eyes the inevitable misfortunes of poor human nature.

The reading of Schlegel and Dennis has taught me to scorn the French critics—Laharpe, Geoffroy, Marmontel—and to scorn all critics. These poor people, unable to create anything, lay a claim to intelligence, and they have no intelligence. For example, the French critics proclaim that Molière is the best of comic authors—present, past, and future. The only truth herein is the first assertion. There is no doubt that

Molière, a man of genius, is superior to that moron admired in the courses of literature whose name is Destouches.

But Molière is inferior to Aristophanes.

Comedy, however, is like music: it is a thing whose beauty *does not last.* The comedy of Molière is too steeped in *satire* to give me very often the sensation of *gay laughter,* if I may so express it. When I go to the theatre for entertainment, I like to encounter a madcap imagination that makes me laugh like a child.

All Louis XIV's subjects prided themselves on imitating a certain model in order to be elegant and *de bon ton;* and Louis XIV himself was the god of that religion. There was a *sarcastic laugh* when one saw another person make a mistake in imitating the model. This accounts for all of the humor in the *Lettres* of Madame de Sévigné. In 1670 a man who, in comedy or in real life, decided to follow quite heedlessly the impulses of a madcap imagination, would not have provoked laughter in the society of the time; he would have passed for a fool.[2]

Molière, a man of genius if there ever was one, had the misfortune to work for that society.

Aristophanes, on the contrary, set out to evoke laughter in a society of amiable and light-hearted people who pursued happiness *in every possible way.* I should imagine that Alcibiades gave very little thought to imitating what was in style. He considered himself happy when he was laughing, and not when he was flushed with pride at feeling himself very similar to Lauzun, d'Antin, Villeroy, or some other famous courtier of Louis XIV.

Our courses in literature have taught us in school that one laughs at Molière; and we believe it, because in France, so far as literature is concerned, we remain schoolboys all our lives. I have undertaken to go to Paris whenever a comedy by Molière or another esteemed author is being performed at the Théâtre-Français. I note in pencil, on the copy of the

[2] The "marketplace theatre" of Regnard, Lesage, and Defresny has no rank in literature. Very few people have read these plays. The same applies to Scarron and Hauteroche.

play I am holding, the exact point at which the audience laughs, and the kind of laughter. For example, there is a laugh when they hear the word "enema" or "cuckolded husband." But this is laughter evoked by the scandalous, and is not the kind Laharpe tells us about.

On December 4, 1822, there was a performance of *Le Tartuffe*. Mlle Mars was appearing. Nothing was lacking for the occasion.

Well! During the whole of *Le Tartuffe* the audience laughed twice—no more. And at that, it was very slight laughter. Several times they applauded the vigor of the satire, or they applauded because of the allusions. But the only times they laughed, on December 4, were:

1. when Orgon, talking to his daughter Marianne about her marriage to Tartuffe (Act II), discovers Dorine nearby, who is listening;

2. during the scene of the quarrel and reconciliation between Valère and Marianne, at a malicious remark made by Dorine on the subject of love.

Astonished that the audience had laughed so little at this masterpiece by Molière, I related what I had observed to a group of intelligent persons. They told me I was mistaken.

Two weeks later I came back to Paris to see *Valérie*. They were also performing *Les Deux gendres*, the famous comedy by M. Etienne. I held my copy and my pencil ready in my hand. The audience laughed exactly *once*. That was when the son-in-law, who is a councilor of state and who is going to become a minister, tells his little cousin that he has read his petition. The spectator laughs because he has very plainly seen the little cousin tear up the petition, which he has seized from the hands of a lackey to whom the councilor of state had given it without reading it.

Unless I am mistaken, the spectator shares the urge toward wild laughter concealed by the little cousin, out of goodness, when he hears himself complimented on the contents of a petition which he knows very well has been torn up without having been read. I told the aforementioned intelligent people that the audience had laughed only this once at *Les Deux gendres*. Their answer was that it was a very good comedy that was excellently composed. So be it! But it therefore follows that laughter is not necessary in order to write a very good French comedy.

Could it be, by any chance, that all one needs is a little action of a very reasonable nature mixed with a rather strong dose of satire, the whole cut up into dialogue and translated into alexandrine lines that are witty, facile, and elegant? If *Les Deux gendres* had been written in vile prose, would it have managed to succeed?

Could it be that because our tragedy is only a series of *odes*[3] interspersed with *epic* narrations[4] that we like to hear declaimed on stage by Talma, in the same way our comedy, since Destouches and Collin d'Harleville, has been only a humorous, subtle, and witty *epistle* that we like to hear read, in the form of dialogue, by Mlle Mars and Damas? [5]

"You have taken us far afield from laughter," the reader will tell me. "You are writing an *ordinary* article on literature, like M.C. in the feuilleton of *Le Journal des débats*."

What do you expect? The trouble is that although I am not yet in the circle of Les Bonnes Lettres,[6] I am ignorant. Moreover, I have taken it upon myself to speak out in the absence of any idea. I hope that this noble audacity will cause me to be received in the circle of Les Bonnes Lettres.

As is very well stated in the German program, an understanding of laughter really requires a dissertation of one hundred and fifty pages. Furthermore, this dissertation must be written in the style of chemistry rather than the academic style.

[3] The monologue of *Le Paria*, of *Régulus*, of *Les Machabées*.
[4] The narrative speeches of Orestes in *Andromaque*. What nation does not have its literary prejudices? Look at the English, who condemn that dull schoolboy exaggeration entitled *Cain: A Mystery*, by Lord Byron, only because it is anti-aristocratic.
[5] It is up to the Paris police to stop the decline of dramatic art. They should make use of their unlimited powers to see that absolutely no free ticket is given out for the first two performances of new plays at the big theatres.
[6] A group that combined political ultraconservatism with literary romanticism of the traditionalist variety. Its members included Chateaubriand, president of the society, and Victor Hugo. [Translator's note.]

Look at those young ladies in the boarding school whose garden can be seen from your windows. They laugh at everything. Is it not perhaps because they see happiness everywhere?

Look at that morose Englishman who has just finished his dinner at Tortoni's. With a bored air, and with the aid of a pince-nez, he is reading voluminous letters that he has received from Liverpool, which have brought him commissions of one hundred thousand francs. That is only half of his annual income; but he doesn't laugh at anything. The fact is that nothing in the world can give him a vision of happiness —not even his position as vice-president of a Bible society.

Regnard's genius is clearly inferior to that of Molière; but I shall make bold to say that he walked in the path of genuine comedy.

Our *student's attitude* toward literature has the result that when we see his comedies, instead of giving ourselves over to his genuinely madcap mirth, we think only of the terrible judgments that have relegated him to the second rank. If we did not know *by heart the very texts* of those severe judgments, we would tremble for our reputations as men of intelligence.

Is this, in all honesty, the proper state of mind for laughter?

As for Molière and his plays, why should I be concerned with the more or less successful imitation of the *bon ton* of the court and the impertinence of the *marquis*?

Today there is no more court. Or at any rate, I have as high an opinion of myself as I do of the persons who go there. And if, after visiting the Stock Exchange and then dining, I go to the theatre, I want somebody to make me laugh; and I never think of imitating anybody.

I want to see candid and brilliant images of all the passions of the human heart—not only and always the graces of the Marquis de Moncade.[7] Today, it is my daughter who is Mademoiselle Benjamine; and I know very well how to reject the marriage offer of a *marquis* if he does not have fifteen thousand *livres* income from landed property. As for his bills of

[7] Of *L'Ecole des Bourgeois.*

30

exchange, if he makes them out and doesn't pay them, M. Mathieu, my brother-in-law, will send him to Sainte-Pélagie.[8] The mere use of the word "Sainte-Pélagie," for a titled man, makes Molière obsolete.

Finally, if they want to make me laugh in spite of the deeply serious state of mind produced in me by the Stock Exchange, politics, and the hatreds of political parties, I require the spectacle of doting persons deceiving themselves, in a humorous way, on the path that leads to happiness.

[8] The prison of Sainte-Pélagie, in Stendhal's day, housed debtors and writers who had been convicted of censorship violations. [Translator's note.]

31

Chapter 3

What Romanticism Is

Romanticism is the art of presenting to different peoples those literary works which, in the existing state of their habits and beliefs, are capable of giving them the greatest possible pleasure.

Classicism, on the contrary, presents to them that literature which gave the greatest possible pleasure to their great-grand-fathers.

Sophocles and Euripides were eminently romantic. To the Greeks assembled in the theatre of Athens, they presented those tragedies which, in accordance with the moral usages of that people, its religion, and its prejudices in the matter of what constitutes the dignity of man, would provide for it the greatest possible pleasure.

To imitate Sophocles and Euripides today, and to maintain that these imitations will not cause a Frenchman of the nineteenth century to yawn with boredom, is classicism.[1]

I do not hesitate to state that Racine was a romantic. He gave the *marquis* of the court of Louis XIV a portrayal of the passions tempered by the *extreme formalism* then in style, which was such that a duke of 1670, even in the most tender effusions of paternal love, never failed to call his son *Monsieur.*

It was for this reason that the Pylades of *Andromaque* always calls Orestes *Seigneur.* And yet how great was the friendship between Orestes and Pylades!

That formalism did not exist at all among the Greeks; and it is because of that formalism, which today we find chilling, that Racine was romantic.

Shakespeare was romantic because he presented to the English of 1590, first, the bloody catastrophes brought on by the civil wars and then, by way of relief from those sad

[1] See the analysis of Greek drama by Metastasio.

spectacles, a wealth of exact portrayals of the emotions and the most delicate nuances of feeling. A hundred years of civil wars and almost continuous troubles, with countless acts of treason, torturings, and generous acts of devotion, had prepared the subjects of Elizabeth for this kind of tragedy, which reproduces almost none of the *artificial* element in the court life and civilization of the tranquil nations. The English of 1590, fortunately very ignorant, loved to contemplate on the stage the image of those misfortunes that had recently been removed from real life thanks to the firm character of their queen. These same fresh details, which our alexandrine lines would repulse with disdain and which are so much appreciated today in *Ivanhoe* and *Rob Roy,* would have seemed to the proud *marquis* of Louis XIV to be lacking in dignity.

Those details would have mortally frightened the sentimental and perfumed dolls who, under Louis XV, could not see a spider without fainting. (This sentence, I realize, is most undignified.)

It requires courage to be a romantic, because one must *take a chance.*

The prudent *classicist,* on the contrary, never takes a step without being supported, secretly, by a line from Homer or by a philosophical comment made by Cicero in his treatise *De Senectute.*

It seems to me that the writer must have almost as much courage as the soldier: the former must give no more thought to the journalists than the latter gives to the hospital.

Lord Byron, the author of some heroic epistles that are sublime but always the same, and of many tragedies that are mortally boring, is not at all the leader of the romantics.

If there existed [sic] a man whose works were the object of strong competitive bidding by the translators in bulk at Madrid, Stuttgart, Paris, and Vienna alike, one could say that such a man had divined the moral trends of his age.[2]

---

[2] This success cannot be a matter of partisanship or personal enthusiasm. At the bottom of all parties there is always a monetary interest. In this case, I can discover only the interest of pleasure. The man himself is hardly deserving of enthusiasm. (His

In France, the popular Pigault-Lebrun is much more romantic than the sensitive author of *Trilby*.

Is there anybody in Brest or Perpignan who rereads *Trilby?*[3]

The romantic element in contemporary tragedy consists in the fact that the playwright always gives a fine role to the devil. He speaks with eloquence and is much admired. People love the opposition.

The antiromantic element is illustrated by M. Legouvé, who in his tragedy of *Henri IV* is unable to reproduce the finest saying of that patriotic king: "It is my wish that the poorest peasant in my kingdom should at least have a chicken in the pot on Sunday."

This truly French saying would have provided a touching scene for even the most poorly endowed student of Shakespeare. But the *Racinian* tragedy puts it much more nobly:

> Je veux enfin qu'au jour marqué pour le repos,
> L'hôte laborieux des modestes hameaux
> Sur sa table moins humble ait, par ma bienfaisance,
> Quelques-uns de ces mets réservés à l'aisance.

(Finally, it is my wish that on the day set aside for repose the laborious dweller in the modest hamlets should, through my beneficence, have on his less humble table some of those dishes reserved for comfortable living.)

La Mort de Henri IV, Act IV[4]

First of all, romantic comedy would not show us characters in embroidered coats. It would not perpetually have lovers and a marriage at the end of the play. The dramatis personae would not change in character precisely in the fifth act. One

---

probable cooperation with the infamous *Beacon*, the ridiculous anecdote about the glass from which George IV had drunk.) [The reference is to Sir Walter Scott. See p. 215. Trans.]

[3] By Charles Nodier (1780-1844), a leader of the French romantic school. [Translator's note.]

[4] In English and Italian verse forms it is possible to say anything. Only the alexandrine line, created for a disdainful court, has all the ridiculous features of the latter.

would sometimes get a glimpse of a love that could not be crowned with marriage. Marriage itself would not be called *hyménée* for the sake of rhyme. (Is there anyone who would not be a laughingstock if he used the word "hymen" in polite society?)

Les Précepteurs, by Fabre d'Eglantine, had opened up a way that censorship has closed. In his *Orange de Malte,* an E. . . [a bishop], they say, was preparing his niece to accept a position as the king's mistress.[5] The only vigorous situation we have seen in twenty years—the scene involving the folding screen in *Le Tartufe de moeurs*—we owe to English drama.[6] In France, anything *strong* is called *indecent.* The audience hissed Molière's *Avare* (February 7, 1823) because of the son's lack of respect for his father.

The most romantic thing in the comedy of our time is not the long plays in five acts, like *Les Deux gendres.* (Show me the person, today, who divests himself of his property.) It is quite simply *Le Solliciteur, Le Ci-devant jeune homme* (copied after Garrick's "Lord Ogleby"),[7] *Michel et Christine, Le Chevalier de Canole, L'Etude du procureur, Les Calicots,* the songs of Béranger, etc. The romantic trend in the burlesque vein is represented by the interrogation in *L'Esturgeon,* from the charming vaudeville by M. Arnault, and by M. Beaufils. There we have the mania for reasoning and the literary Dandinism[8] of our age.

M. l'abbé Delille was eminently romantic for the age of Louis XV. His was, indeed, the kind of poetry suitable for the people who, at Fontenoy, took off their hats to the English

---

[5] It was customary, in speaking to Madame de Pompadour, to refer to the *position* that she occupied. See the *Mémoires* of Bézenval, Marmontel, and Madame d'Epinay. These *Mémoires* are replete with strong situations, in no way indecent, that our timid comedy does not dare to reproduce. See the story, *Le Spleen,* by Bézenval.

[6] *Le Tartufe de moeurs,* by Louis-Claude Chéron (1758-1807) was an imitation of Sheridan's *School for Scandal.* [Translator's note.]

[7] Presumably a reference to *The Clandestine Marriage,* by Garrick and Colman. [Translator's note.]

[8] After Pierre Dandin, the judge in *Pantagruel,* who decides cases summarily and stupidly. [Translator's note.]

column and said: "Fire first, gentlemen." This is assuredly very noble. But how do such people have the effrontery to say that they admire Homer?

The ancients would have had a good laugh at our sense of honor.

And they expect that this poetry will be to the liking of a Frenchman who participated in the retreat from Moscow! [9]

No people in the memory of an historian has undergone a more rapid and complete change in its morals and pleasures than that from 1780 to 1823. And they want to give us the same literature as before!

Our solemn adversaries should take a look around them. The fool of 1780 produced stupid, flat jokes. He was always laughing. The fool of 1823 produces philosophical arguments that are vague, repetitious, and terribly dull. And he always wears a long face. Here we have a very important revolution. A society in which an element so essential and constant as the *fool* has changed to this extent can no longer put up with the same ridiculous things or the same pathetic ones. In those days everybody tried to make the other person laugh. Today everybody wants to deceive the other person.

An atheistic attorney buys the works of Bourdaloue[10] in a magnificent binding and says: "This is suitable for the clerks."

The romantic poet *par excellence* is Dante. He venerated Vergil; and yet he wrote *The Divine Comedy* and the episode of Ugolino, which of all things in the world least resembles *The Aeneid*. This was because he understood that in his time people were afraid of Hell.

The romantics do not advise anybody to imitate the plays of Shakespeare directly.

What one should imitate in that great man is his manner of studying the world we live in and the art of giving to our

[9] M. Lemercier's *Panhypocrisiade,* if it were not so badly written, would be the poem of the age. Just imagine the "Battlefield of Pavia" translated into French by Boileau or M. l'abbé Delille. In this poem of four hundred pages, there are forty verses more striking and more beautiful than any by Boileau.

[10] A prominent churchman of Louis XIV's time, renowned for his skill as an orator and for the sermons that constitute his *Works.* [Translator's note.]

contemporaries precisely the kind of tragedy they need but do not have the boldness to demand, because they are so terrified by the reputation of the great Racine.

The new French tragedy might by chance bear a strong resemblance to that of Shakespeare.

But this would be only because our circumstances are the same as those of England in 1590. We, too, have factions, tortures, and plots. Someone who is now laughing, as he reads this pamphlet in a salon, will be in prison within a week. Another person, who is joking with him, will name the jury that will convict him.

We would soon have the *new French tragedy* that I am bold enough to predict if we had a strong enough feeling of security to take an active interest in literature. I say "feeling of security" because the trouble is especially in people's imaginations, which are given to fears. In the countryside and on the main roads, we have a physical security that would have been most astonishing to the England of 1590.

Because in the matter of intelligence, we are infinitely superior to the English of that age, our new tragedy will have more simplicity. Shakespeare employs rhetoric continually. This is because he had to make the situations in his drama comprehensible to an uncouth public with more courage than subtlety.

Our new tragedy will strongly resemble *Pinto*, the masterpiece of M. Lemercier.

The French mentality will especially reject the German bombast that many people today call romantic.

Schiller *copied* Shakespeare and his rhetoric. He lacked the intelligence to give his fellow countrymen the kind of tragedy required by their social usages.

I was forgetting the *unity of place*. It will be swept away in the rout of the alexandrine.

M. Picard's pleasant comedy *Le Conteur,* which only needs to have been written by Beaumarchais or Sheridan in order to be delicious, has given the public the good habit of realizing that there exist charming subjects for which changes of scenery are absolutely necessary.

We are almost as far advanced in the matter of tragedy.

How does it happen that the Emilie of *Cinna* comes to the emperor's council chamber to do her conspiring? How can one imagine *Sylla* performed without changing the sets?

If M. Chénier had lived, that intelligent man would have rid us of the unity of place in tragedy and, consequently, of boring narrative speeches. He would have rid us of that unity of place that makes it forever impossible to dramatize great national subjects: the assassination of Montereau, the Etats de Blois, the death of Henri III.

Henri III requires absolutely, on the one hand Paris, the Duchess of Montpensier, and the cloister of the Jacobin friars, and on the other Saint-Cloud, the irresolution, the weakness, the sensual pleasures, and suddenly death, which puts an end to the whole thing.

Racinian tragedy can never use more than the thirty-six hours of an action; hence, there is never any development of the passions. What plot has the time to be hatched, or what movement of the people can develop, in thirty-six hours?

It is interesting, it is *beautiful,* to see Othello, so much in love in the first act, kill his wife in the fifth. If this change were to take place in thirty-six hours, it would be absurd, and I would have only contempt for Othello.

Macbeth, a good man in the first act, is enticed by his wife, murders his king and benefactor, and becomes a bloody monster. Either I am mistaken, or these changes of the passions in the human heart are the most magnificent thing that poetry can hold up to be viewed by the eyes of men, whom it at once moves and instructs.

The Naïveté of the *Journal des Débats* (Feuilleton of July 8, 1818)

. . . O happy days when the theatre pit was occupied almost entirely by devoted and studious young people whose memory was *adorned in advance* with all the beautiful lines of Racine and Voltaire; young people who went to the theatre *only to round out the pleasure of their reading!* [11]

[11] An excerpt from an article in the *Journal des débats*. [Translator's note.]

Résumé

I am far from claiming that M. David ranks higher than the Lebruns and the Mignards. In my opinion, the modern artist, more remarkable for his strength of character than for his talent, remains inferior to the great painters of the age of Louis XIV. But what would MM. Gros, Girodet, Guérin, Prudhon, and all the distinguished painters produced by his school be today had it not been for M. David? Perhaps more or less ridiculous Vanloos and Buchers.

On Molière, Regnard, and Other Matters [1]

A few persons who had the kindness to read this pamphlet in its entirety have told the author that his ideas seemed to have particularly little relevance to Molière. It is quite possible that a man of genius writing works which are very pleasurable to people in one era of civilization should still give more pleasure to the people of a totally different era than do the mediocre artists of this latter age. These mediocre artists are boring chiefly because they slavishly copy the works of the great man. They are incapable of seeing either life as it exists before their very eyes, or life as it was when the great man gave us his sublime imitations of it.

I have deemed it appropriate to write a new chapter on Molière; and I have entered into a few serious bits of reasoning, at the risk of seeming heavy.

This pamphlet has brought me an honor of which I am proud. A few of those men whose writings, and not their evening visions [visits?], *have earned them a leading place in literature—a few of those men whose writings lend pleasure to my hours of leisure—have deigned to offer some objections to what I have said. I have taken the risk of replying to those objections with a new chapter. If I had allowed myself to voice my self-doubts as often as I feel how many reasons I have to be modest, this additional chapter would have been very long. I have so far respected my noble adversaries as to believe that they would have enough pride to love the truth without formulas. And I have therefore spoken simply, as one speaks to the immortals, saying in a plain way not what is true, perhaps, but what seems to me to be true.*

[1] The chapters grouped under this heading were apparently intended by Stendhal to serve as a supplement to the three chapters of the first *Racine and Shakespeare* pamphet (1823), *supra,* and were so treated by Colomb in his 1854 edition of the work. The "chapter" on French declamation (three paragraphs) has been omitted here. [Translator's note.]

Chapter 4

On the State of Society with Respect to Comedy in the Reign of Louis XIV

To HATE SOMETHING is not a pleasure. In fact I believe many readers will agree with me that it is painful; and the more imagination or sensitivity one has, the greater the pain.

La Bruyère said: "To escape from the court for a single moment is to give it up. The courtier who has seen it in the morning sees it in the evening in order to recognize it the next day and in order that he himself be recognized there."

Even in 1670, in the best days of Louis XIV, the court was merely an assemblage of enemies and rivals. It was dominated by hatred and envy. How could true gaiety have shown itself there?

Those people who hated one another so cordially and who died after fifty years of hate still inquiring on their deathbed, "How is Monsieur So-and-So?" [2]—those people detested even more certain human beings of whom they never took notice except to oppress them or to be afraid of them. Their hatred was all the stronger in that it was preceded by contempt. There was nothing in the world that could shock them so much as the suspicion that they had something in common with such people. "What you have just said is very common," said Louis XIV one day when that great king deemed it appropriate to carry reprimand almost to the point of insult. In the eyes of Louis XIV, Henri IV, or Louis XVIII there were never more than two classes of people in France: the nobles, who had to be governed by *honor* and recompensed with the *cordon bleu;*[3] and the *canaille,* to whom one threw sausages and hams on great occasions, but whom it was

[2] Factual. See Saint-Simon.
[3] The decoration worn by members of the order called "The Knights of the Holy Ghost." [Translator's note.]

41

necessary to hang or massacre without pity the moment they took it into their heads to express their opinions.[4]

This state of civilization offered two sources of comedy for the courtiers: first, when a person made a mistake in imitating what was in good taste at court; second, when a person's manners or conduct showed some resemblance to a bourgeois. The letters of Madame de Sévigné prove all these things to the point of obviousness. She was a gentle, amiable, moderate woman, not at all malicious. (See her correspondence during her sojourns at her estate, Les Rochers, and the tone in which she talks about the hangings and other harsh measures employed by her good friend, the Duke of Chaulnes.)

These charming letters show above all that a courtier was always poor. He was poor because he could not have the same luxuries as his neighbor. And what was really *frightful* and painful for him was the favor of the court, which made it possible for that neighbor to display all this sumptuousness.

And so, in addition to the two sources of hatred mentioned above, the courtier also had (to contribute to his happiness) poverty plus vanity—the cruelest of all, because it is followed by contempt.[5]

At the court of Louis XIV, in 1670, among so many bitter sorrows, disappointed hopes, and betrayed friendships, one last resort remained for those vain and frivolous souls: the anxiety of the gamble, the raptures of winning, the horror of losing. Consider the profound desolation of a Vardes or a Bussy-Rabutin in the depths of this exile. To be no longer at court was to have all the misfortunes and sorrows, and to feel all the sharp edges, of the civilization of that day, without having the things that made them bearable. In exile, one had either to live with bourgeois (a horrible thing) or to see courtiers of the third or fourth rank who came to the province to discharge their duties, and who bestowed their

[4] The *Mémoires* of Bassompierre, de Gourville, *et al.*
[5] The letters of Madame de Sévigné. Details on the life and projects of M. le marquis de Sévigné and MM. de Grignan, father and son.

pity upon one. The masterpiece of Louis XIV, the comple-
ment of the system of Richelieu, was to create this desolation
of exile.

For anyone who knows how to view it, the court of Louis
XIV was never anything more than a game of faro. It was
people like this whom, in the intervals between games,
Molière undertook to amuse. He succeeded like the great man
that he was; that is, almost perfectly. The comedies that he
produced for the courtiers of the *sun-king* were probably
the best and the most amusing that one could write for such
people. But, in 1825, we are no longer this kind of people.
Public opinion is formed by people living in Paris, with more
than ten thousand *livres* of income and less than one hundred.

Sometimes the formalism[6] of Louis XIV's courtiers was
shocked even by the humorous imitation of what was most
ridiculously odious in their eyes: a merchant of Paris. The
Bourgeois gentilhomme struck them as frightful, not because
of the role of Dorante, which today would give the chills to
MM. Auger, Lémontey, and other censors, but quite simply
because it was degrading and disgusting to have their eyes
fixed for so long on a being so abject as M. Jourdain—on a
merchant of Paris. Still, Louis XIV had better taste. That
great king wanted to raise up those of his subjects engaged
in industry. And by one remark he made them worthy of
being mocked. "Molière," he said to his valet-upholsterer,
who was plunged into sadness by the contempt of the court,
"Molière, you never yet wrote anything which amused me so
much. Your play is excellent."

I must confess that I am not deeply touched by this act of
charity on the part of the great king.

When, about 1720, the dissipations of the great lords and
the system devised by Law had finally created a bourgeoisie,
a third source of comedy appeared: the imperfect and awk-

[6] In order to get an exact idea of this formalism, see the *Mémoires*
of the Duchess of Orléans, the mother of the Regent. This sincere
German woman casts a bit of doubt upon the countless lies of
Madame de Genlis, M. de Lacretelle, and other persons of the
same weight.

ward imitation of those amiable courtiers. The son of M. Turcaret,[7] who took the disguise of a *nom de terre* and became a farmer-general of the king's revenues, must have led the kind of social life[8] for which there had been no model under Louis XIV, in that century when the ministers themselves had been only bourgeois to start with. A courtier could see M. Colbert only on business matters. Paris became filled with very wealthy bourgeois whose names you will find in the *Mémoires* of Collé: MM. d'Angivilliers, Turgot, Trudaine, Monticourt, Helvétius, d'Epinay, *et al.* Little by little these opulent and well-bred men, the sons of vulgar men like Turcaret, brought into being that fatal public opinion which finally spoiled everything in 1789. These farmers-general entertained men of letters at their *soupers,* and the latter emerged somewhat from the role of *buffoons* that they had played at the tables of the real *grands seigneurs.*

Duclos' *Considérations sur les moeurs* constitutes the Civil Code for this new order, a rather amusing description of which has been given to us in the *Mémoires* of Madame d'Epinay and Marmontel. We are told of a M. de Bellegarde who, despite his great name, is only a farmer-general. But he spends two hundred thousand francs a year. And his son, reared in the same luxury as the Duke of Fronsac, feels he is the latter's equal in manners.[9]

[7] This evening my carriage was held up for a quarter of an hour on the Boulevard des Italiens by the descendants of Crusaders, who were standing in line in order to gain admission to a ball given by a Jewish banker (M. de Rothschild). The noble ladies of the Faubourg Saint-Germain had spent the early part of the day in all kinds of base maneuvers so that they might be invited.

[8] The *Mémoires* of Collé.

[9] Madame d'Epinay's morning reception: "The two liveried servants open the swinging doors so that I can pass through, and shout to the people in the reception room, 'Madame is coming, Messieurs. Madame is coming!' Everyone lines up. First in line is some young scamp who has come to bellow an aria. After having given him some lessons in good taste and having taught him what it is to sing French correctly, I grant him my patronage so that he can have entree into the Opéra. Then there are drapers, persons dealing in musical instruments, jewelers, peddlers, bootblacks, creditors, lackeys, etc. (*Mémoires et correspondance de Madame d'Epinay,* Vol. I, pp. 356–57.)

From this moment, Turcaret was without models. But this new society of the period between 1720 and 1790, this total change so important in history and politics, was of hardly any importance for comedy. During all this time, comedy produced no man of genius. Astonished at being able to reason, people pursued this altogether new pleasure at a furious pace. To reason on the existence of God seemed something fascinating, even to the ladies. The *parlements* and the archbishops, by means of their condemnations, added something piquant to this arid way of employing one's intelligence. Everybody was avidly reading *Emile,* the *Encyclopédie,* and *The Social Contract.*

One man of genius appeared at the very end of this period. The Academy, through the medium of M. Suard's publication, condemned Beaumarchais. But it was no longer a matter of amusing oneself in a salon. People were already thinking of rebuilding the house; and the architect Mirabeau won out over the decorator Beaumarchais. When a modicum of good faith in governmental power has brought the revolution to an end, everything will fall into place little by little. Heavy, philosophical, and unassailable reasoning will be left to the Chamber of Deputies. When this happens, comedy will be reborn, because people will have a wild urge to laugh.

The hypocrisy of the old Madame de Maintenon and of the old age of Louis XIV was followed by the orgies of the Regent. Likewise, when at last we emerge from this lugubrious farce and are permitted to dispense with passports, rifles, epaulettes, Jesuits' robes, and the whole revolutionary paraphernalia, we shall have an era of charming gaiety.

But let us abandon these political conjectures and return to comedy. In the mediocre comedies between 1720 and 1790, one was ridiculous when one did not imitate in the approved manner those usages of the court that M. de Monticourt or M. de Trudaine, who were wealthy men of Paris, could allow their vanity.[10]

But I am a Frenchman of 1825, who enjoys esteem in proportion to his wealth and pleasures in proportion to his wit.

[10] The role of Récard in a five-act prose comedy of Collé following his *Mémoires;* the Mondor of *Les Fausses infidélités,* etc.

What does the more or less successful imitation of the *bon ton* of the court mean to me? It is still necessary, in order to be ridiculous, that a person make a false step on the road to happiness. But happiness no longer consists, for the French, merely in imitating (each according to established usages) the manners of the court.

Nonetheless, it should be noted that we have retained the habit of conforming, in our acts, to an accepted model. No people is so tenacious of its habits as the French. The key to this mystery is an excess of vanity: we abhor hidden dangers.

Still and all, we are no longer in the time of Louis XIV and his arrogant courtiers (so well depicted by another courtier, Dangeau), who were responsible for fabricating the *model* to which everyone, in accordance with the rules of decorum applicable to his station, was terribly anxious to conform.

It is the *opinion of the majority* that erects in the public square the model to which everyone scrupulously conforms. It is no longer enough to take a false step on the road that leads to the court. Count Alfieri, in his autobiography, relates the following. On New Year's Day, 1768, the aldermen of Paris lost their way and did not arrive at the gallery of Versailles in time to receive the glance that Louis XV deigned to throw in their direction. On that New Year's Day, on his way to Mass, the king asked what had become of the aldermen. A voice replied, "They are still stuck in the mud." And the king himself deigned to smile.[11]

Anecdotes of this kind are still told; and in the Faubourg Saint-Germain people laugh at them as they would at a fairy tale. They still have a bit of nostalgia for the fairy days. But there are two centuries between those poor aldermen of Paris, getting bogged down in the mud on the road to Versailles, and great lords coming to seek a bourgeois reputation for eloquence in the Chamber of Deputies, so that they can move on from there to a ministry.

[11] *Vita di Alfieri,* Vol. I, p. 140.

Chapter 5

On Conversation

COURTIERS OF ALL ERAS have had one need resulting from their status: that of talking without saying anything. This was a great advantage for Molière. His comedies provided a pleasant supplement to the events of the daily hunt—to the elegant exclamations on the wiles of the stag, and to the raptures of admiration for the king's skill in horseback riding.

Our conversation is in a very different state: we have only too many interesting things to say. Art no longer consists in husbanding a meager source of interest that is always on the point of petering out—in making it suffice for everything and enlivening the most arid dissertations. On the contrary, we have to restrain a torrent of deep feelings, ready to burst forth at every word and threatening to upset all decorum and scatter far afield the denizens of the salon. We have to avoid subjects so interesting that they are irritating. The great art of conversation, today, is not to wallow in the *odious*.

Accustomed as we are to reasoning often in conversation, we would find pedantic and definitely odd—if we dared to reason by ourselves like big boys—the conversation of the *marquis* in the second act of *Le Misanthrope*. It is probably true that a century ago this scene presented a faithful picture (and one idealized by genius) of the salons of 1670. We can see that it offered a rather good opening for satire, and that the court of Louis XIV was very much *small town*. The fact is that in every country, *gossip* is engendered by a lack of ideas.

Ten character sketches, which are piquant but which might just as easily occur in a satire of Boileau,[1] are presented successively to our view.

---

[1] The garrulous individual who tries to keep the attention of everybody in the salon; the *raisonneur* who only succeeds in being boring; the man of mystery; the person given to familiarity who finds

We have taken a step forward since 1670, although we are careful not to admit it. We would almost concede, if urged to do so in a gracious manner, that it is all very fine for all those people to have manias, if their manias amuse them. The philosophy of the eighteenth century has taught us that a bird should not mock a mole because of the dark tunnel in which the latter chooses to live. The mole probably enjoys itself in its tunnel: it makes love there, and it lives there.

As for Alceste, the misanthropist, his position is different. He is in love with Célimène and tries to please her. A mole should not stay in its hole if it has undertaken to pay court to a nightingale.

The brilliant Célimène, a young widow of twenty, amuses herself at the expense of the ridiculous traits in her friends. But in her salon, everyone is careful not to mention the odious. Alceste lacks this prudence; and this is precisely what constitutes the particular ridiculousness of that unfortunate young man. His mania for seizing upon everything that seems odious; his talent for accurate and concise reasoning; and his severe probity—all this would soon lead to politics, or what is even worse, to a seditious and obnoxious philosophy. If that were to happen, Célimène's salon would become compromising. It would soon be a desert. And what can a coquette do in an empty salon?

This is why Alceste's kind of discourse was in bad taste in her salon. And this is what Philinte should have told him. It was the duty of that judicious friend of Alceste to oppose the latter's passion to his mania for reasoning. Molière saw it more clearly than we can. But the evidence and the pertinence of Philinte's reasoning might have cost the playwright the great king's favor.

---

it charming to use intimate language with everybody; the malcontent who feels the king has done him an injustice every time he grants a favor; the man who, like a minister, founds his success on nothing more than his cook; the peremptory talker who tries to judge everything, and who would feel he had lowered himself if he offered the slightest evidence for the decrees he pronounces from the loftiness of his pride.

On the other hand, the great king must have found that the ridicule heaped upon a mania for serious reasoning was in very good taste.[2]

The *odious* thing that we avoid today is of another kind. It is in bad taste only when it leads to a feeling of impotent rage. And it is pleasant as soon as it can take the form of amusing ridicule aimed at persons in power. Not only that, but the more august the rank of the persons ridiculed, the more pleasure yielded by the witticism, rather than causing any fear whatsoever:

"The Council of Ministers has just adjourned. It lasted for three hours."

"What happened? [*Que s'est-il passé?*]"

"Three hours happened. [*Il s'est passé trois heures.*] That idiotic old minister doesn't want to open his eyes to anything."

"Well, then, let him close them!"[3]

After a reign of a century, a lively kind of conversation—pleasant, sparkling with wit, always simulating gaiety and avoiding a serious tone as the most ridiculous of things—was suddenly dethroned, about 1786, by heavy, interminable discussion in which all the fools take part. Today, they all have their judgment to pass on Napoleon, and we have to endure them. Horseback riding, visits in informal morning dress, and the activities of the morning have given way to the newspapers. In 1786, one had to give two hours of one's life, every day, to avid reading, punctuated almost every moment by exclamations of hatred or sarcastic laughter at the humiliating disappointments of the enemy camp. French frivolity, however, has perished and been replaced by solemnity

---

[2] If there ever was a man born to inspire in others, through his own gentleness, a love of wisdom, it was Franklin without any doubt. And yet just to look at the very odd place in which Louis XVI had his portrait put, to send it to the Duchess of Polignac. (*Mémoires* of Madame Campan.) The "odd place" was a chamber pot. [Translator's note.]

[3] The *Miroir* (a little newspaper which is very liberal and very witty), March, 1823.

49

—to such an extent that the amiable people of another century are conspicuous in the salons of 1825.

France being without universities according to the German pattern, conversation used to constitute the entire education of a Frenchman. Today, it is conversation and the newspapers.

Chapter 6

Concerning Living Habits, with Respect to Literature

I SEE PEOPLE of my acquaintance spending six months of the year in the idleness of the countryside. The tranquility of the country has replaced the anxiety of the courts and the agitation of life in Paris.[1] The husband sees to the cultivation of his land; the wife says she is enjoying herself; and the children are happy. With no need of new ideas coming from Paris, they run and frolic in the woods. They lead the life of nature.

To tell the truth, people like this have learned from their fathers to say that they are shocked by the least lack of decorum in products of the intellect; that they are repelled when the slightest rule of good manners is violated. The fact is that since they are very bored and totally lacking in new and amusing ideas, they devour the worst kind of novels. The booksellers are well aware of this. Everything that is just too dull during the rest of the year, they set aside for the month of April—the great time for packing up and going to the country.

Thus *boredom* has already broken all of the rules for the novel. *Boredom!* that god I implore! The mighty god who reigns in the Théâtre-Français; the only power in the world that can make people throw Laharpe into the fire. Anyway, the revolution in the novel was easy. Our pedants, finding that the Greeks and the Romans did not write novels, decreed that this genre was beneath their wrath. This is why the novel has been sublime. What tragedians following the precepts of Aristotle have produced, in the past century, anything to compare to *Tom Jones, Werther,* the *Tableaux de famille,*

[1] The *Mémoires* of Madame d'Epinay; the life led by M. de Francueil, her lover.

51

La Nouvelle Héloïse, or *Old Mortality?* Just compare these to the contemporary French tragedies. (You will find the melancholy list of the latter in Grimm.)

Back in the city at the end of November, our rich people, bored to death with six months of domestic felicity, would like nothing better than to enjoy themselves at the theatre. They rejoice at the mere sight of the entrance to the Théâtre-Français, because they have forgotten the boredom of the year before. But at the door they encounter a terrible monster: *prudery,* to put it plainly.

In everyday life, prudery is the art of taking offense on account of virtues that one does not possess. In literature, it is the art of affecting tastes that one does not possess. This artificial existence makes us praise *Les Femmes savantes* to the skies and scorn the charming *Retour imprévu.*

Upon uttering these offensive words, I see anger in the eyes of the classicists. Just a moment, gentlemen! You shouldn't get angry except about something that really angers you. Is anger such a pleasant sensation?

"No, certainly not. But when we frown at the farces of Regnard, we advance our reputations as good *littérateurs.*"

It looks, then, as though *le bon ton* has become very common, because there is no shop clerk who does not hiss Molière or Regnard at least once a year. This is just as natural for him as assuming the military bearing of a wrathful drum major when he walks into a café. It is said that prudery is the virtue of women who have no virtue. Could it not very well be that *literary prudery* is the *good taste* of people whom nature created for no other purpose than to appreciate money or have a passionate fondness for stuffed turkey?

One of the most deplorable consequences of this century's corruption is that the comedy of society no longer deceives anyone in literature. If some affected man of letters still succeeds in creating an illusion, it is only because people hold him in too much contempt to look twice.

The most fortunate thing for literature under Louis XIV was the fact that in those days it was nothing of any great importance.[2] The courtiers who judged the masterpieces of Racine and Molière used good taste because they had no idea they were acting as judges. Whereas in their manners and their dress they were always careful to imitate somebody, in their thinking about literature they dared to be quite frankly themselves. But "dared" is not the word. They didn't even have to take the trouble to *dare*. Literature was only a bagatelle of no importance. *Having correct opinions about works of literature*[3] did not become essential to social esteem until the latter part of the reign of Louis XIV, when literature inherited some of the high esteem that king had accorded to the Racines and the Despréaux.

One always judges well those things one judges naturally. Everyone is right in his own taste, however whimsical, because it is a vote by heads. The error creeps in the moment one says: "My taste is that of the majority, the general taste, *good taste.*"

Even a *pedant,* judging *naturally* in accordance with his narrow, petty soul, would have the right to be heard. Because, after all, he is a spectator; and the playwright wants to please all the spectators. The pedant becomes ridiculous only when he begins to judge with an acquired taste and when he tries to convince you that he has subtle perceptions, feelings, etc. For example, Laharpe commenting on *Le Cid* and the rigors of the *point d'honneur* after climbing out of a creek into which he had been tossed by a certain Blin de Sainmore, one day when the academician, all dressed up, was on his way to dinner at the home of a farmer-general. They say that the commentator of *Le Cid,* although his clothes were a bit muddy, put on a very good countenance at the dinner table.

One of the most amusing consequences of *prudery* is that, like oligarchy, it always tends to purge itself of impure ele-

---

[2] "The old man Corneille died a few days ago," Dangeau said. Today, four speeches would be given at the Père-Lachaise Cemetery and published the next day in *Le Moniteur.*
[3] The title of a work of a Jesuit of those days (Bouhours, I believe), which enjoyed a great success.

ments. And a faction that purges itself is soon reduced to the *divan of the doctrinaires*.[4]

It is impossible to say just how far the refinement of language would have gone if the reign of Louis XIV had continued. Even in his day, M. l'abbé Delille could use no more than half the words that La Fontaine had used. Everything natural would soon have became vulgar and base. Before long, there would not have been one thousand persons in all of Paris who spoke nobly.

I will not cite examples which are too old for anyone to remember. Just two years ago (February, 1823), when it was a question of liberating Spain and giving back to her that happiness which she enjoys today, did not some of the salons in the Faubourg Saint-Germain find M. de Talleyrand's speech in bad taste? Now I ask you: Who can flatter himself that he has good diction if a man so well bred, whom no one will accuse of having avoided court life, can be accused of bad taste in his style? Upon close examination, one can discover as many as three or four different kinds of diction in Paris. Language that is crude in the Faubourg Saint-Dominique is merely natural in the Faubourg Saint-Honoré and runs the risk of seeming affected in the Rue du Mont-Blanc. But the written language, which is intended to be understood by everybody, and not just in the Oeil-de-Boeuf, should have no concern with these fashions of the moment.

It is *affectation* which hisses Molière three times a month. Otherwise one could predict that it will soon be improper and in bad taste to say, on the French stage: "Close that window."

I believe it is already time to say: "Close that window." [5] But that poor thing, *prudery*, despite its *Journal des débats*, and despite its Académie Française recruited by government

---

[4] The *canapé des doctrinaires* was a term applied, under the Restoration, to a political faction which had become so small that, according to a wit of the day, all of its members could sit on one sofa. [Translator's note.]

[5] Possibly a pun on the word *croisée*, meaning both "window" and (archaically) "crusade." (Let's call a halt to this crusade.") [Translator's note.]

order, is wounded in the heart and will not go very much further. Please note that this excessive refinement *exists only in the theatre* and is supported only by the *Journal des débats.* It has already disappeared from our manners and morals. The influx of people from the provinces, who come to sit in the Chamber of Deputies, has had the result that in conversation we usually talk to make ourselves understood.[6]

[6] Reflections of M. Alexandre Duval on the style of comedy in the nineteenth century. Three-fourths of the charming witticisms of Lord Byron, in *Don Juan,* and especially in "The Age of Bronze," would be vulgar in French. And they come from the most lofty and disdainful genius of England.

Chapter 7

Concerning Scenes Depicting Manners in Terms of Strong Situations, and the *Vis Comica*

THE COURT OF LOUIS XIV put a heavy strain on the shrewdness of the courtier. Every morning he had to detect, from the look in the master's eyes, whether his favor was on the wane, or whether it would continue at all. Because the least gesture was decisive, the slightest nuance was observed.

The republic, on the contrary, has engendered the art of discussion, serious attacks, and the *eloquence of the rostrum* intended to stir up the masses. The knavery of a cabinet minister is always rather easy to see. The difficult thing is to make it tangible in the eyes of the people and arouse public indignation about it. It requires good sense and patience to detect a duplicated item in the friendly shade of a budget.[1] It required charming manners, a lively intellect, a high degree of tact attuned to the slightest nuance, and shrewdness at every moment to win or keep the favor of a despot who was bored and had a most refined taste,[2] because for fifty years he had been flattered by the most amiable men of Europe. Those courtiers who, every morning, went to read their fate in the eyes of the king, decided in their turn the fate of those who paid court to them and to whom they transmitted the same habits of perception. Before long this habit became general among all the French.

Molière, with his genius, was quick to note this deep shrewdness among the members of his audiences; and he made use of it for their pleasure and for his own fame. His plays are full of *testing* scenes, if I may so designate scenes

[1] Mr. Hume, in England, in the House of Commons, before Mr. Canning conceived the idea of resorting to good faith to keep himself in office.
[2] The *Lettres* of Madame de Maintenon.

which *test* the character or passions of the persons involved. Need I recall lines like "The poor man!" which is so fashionable today. Or "Oh God, forgive him his sins as I forgive him!" [3] Or Harpagon's "Without a dowry!" Or "How did he ever get into *that* fix?" from *Les Fourberies de Scapin.* Or "You are in the trade, Monseiur Josse." Or Orgon's "Get thee behind me, rascal!" to his son, Damis, who has just accused the good M. Tartuffe. These are celebrated witticisms which have enriched the language.

This is what many classical *littérateurs* call the *vis comica,* without stopping to realize that there is nothing comical in seeing Orgon curse and drive off his son, who has just accused Tartuffe of an obvious crime—and this because Tartuffe replies with phrases lifted from the Catechism, which prove nothing. The eye suddenly looks into one of the depths of the human heart—but a depth that is more curious than laughable. We see a good man, like Orgon, let himself be convinced by phrases that prove nothing. We are too attentive—I would even go so far as to say, too deeply moved— to laugh. We see that there is nothing so difficult to prove as the obvious, because the people who need to have it proven to them are blind. We see that the evident truth, our great support in acting on other men (because one must necessarily convince those whom one does not command) and the means of support by which we often move ahead to happiness, can suddenly fail us at the moment when we need it most urgently. A fact of this kind presages danger of a sort. And as soon as *danger* enters the picture, there is no longer any question of that frivolous comparison which produces laughter. [4]

This certainly represents strength, or *vis.* But why add the word *comica* (that which causes laughter) if no one laughs? *Vis comica* is one of the expressions of the old *classical* literature.

Shakespeare's "Misanthropist," entitled *Timon of Athens,*

[3] The death of the poor old man, Llorente, in 1823.
[4] This is the sentiment whose lack makes kings into nitwits. They never, or only very rarely, *have to persuade anybody of anything.* Hence the difficulty in persuading themselves.

is full of very strong and very beautiful scenes. But no one laughs at them. This is because they are only *testing* scenes, if I may be permitted this expression. In those scenes the character of the misanthropist is established, for the spectator, in a manner superior to any objection—and not on hearsay or the accounts of men-servants, but on the basis of incontestable proofs: things that take place before the spectator's very eyes.

The bad-tempered Ménechme, in the comedy of that name, is the amusing misanthropist; and Regnard appropriated him for his own use. But poor Regnard, who was always gay, like the manners and morals of the Regency or of Venice, gives us scarcely any *testing* scenes. He would have found them boring or sad.

And so these scenes, which are strong but not comical, yield a very great philosophical pleasure. Old men like to quote them and then mentally classify all the events of their lives—which proves that Molière had accurate insight into the depths of the human heart. We often think of these immortal scenes, and we allude to them constantly. In conversation, they always cap our ideas. For the person who knows how to quote them apropos, they are by turns judgments, axioms, or jokes. No other scenes will ever penetrate so far into the French mentality. In this sense, they are like the religions: the time for creating them has passed. Finally, it is probably more difficult to write such scenes than to write the amusing scenes of Regnard. Orgon, seizing Tartuffe just when the latter, after having taken a good look around the entire room, has embraced Elmire, presents a spectacle full of genius but not comical. This scene strikes the spectator. It strikes him with helpless amazement, and it *avenges* him, if you will; but *it does not make him laugh.*

If someone will find another expression of admiration for Molière—for example: "He is the French poet with the 'most genius' "—I will gladly subscribe to it. And furthermore, I have always thought so. But let us not be dazzled by a great man. Let us not lend him qualities he does not possess. Should one admire base despotism because its throne has been adorned by a man like Napoleon?

However great Molière is, *Regnard is more comical*. He makes me laugh more often, and more heartily—and that despite the great inferiority of his genius. Imagine how far Molière would have gone if he had written for the court of the Regent, instead of living in the reign of Louis XIV! It is in vain that Boileau says:

> Dans le sac ridicule où Scapin s'enveloppe,
> Je ne reconnais plus l'auteur du Misanthrope

(In the ludicrous bag in which Scapin wraps himself, I no longer recognize the author of *Le Misanthrope*.)

I leave to poor Boileau, the poet of reason, his decorum of a bourgeois admitted to the court of Louis XIV, and his natural coldness.

The comedy of *Le Misanthrope* is like a splendid and magnificent palace built at great expense, where I grow bored—where time does not move. *Les Fourberies* is a pretty little country house, a charming cottage, where my heart is gladdened, and where I give no thought to anything grave.

On every occasion after I have laughed at *Le Ci-devant jeune homme* or *Le Solliciteur* at the Variétés, I leave the theatre in a rage against our petty rhetoricians who will not allow Ymbert and Scribe to write five-act comedies for the Théâtre-Français, and to develop at leisure those subjects of ridicule which today they can only touch upon in passing.

Will no one step forward to dethrone the pedants? Shall we once again let them falsify the taste of those fine young people who applaud with such noble enthusiasm the eloquent lessons of the Cousins and the Daunous? They are so little deceived by political disguises: will they always remain the dupes of literary disguises? Just once, before taking my leave of this world, I would like to laugh at a new play at the Théâtre-Français. Is this asking too much? And those gentlemen of the Academy, who constitute *a class* and whom one can no longer make fun of except at the risk of going to prison—will they always stop us from laughing, even when we are not in any way thinking of their brilliant qualities?

Chapter 8

On the Morality of Molière

ALTHOUGH I FIND scarcely worthy of attention everything that narrow-minded persons have said about the *morality* of the theatre, it is easy to see that Molière is no more moral than anybody else. This argument in his favor must be banished along with that other old-fashioned notion of "the beauty of the morality of religions." The essential thing, which nobody mentions, is to create interests that incline people to follow certain good moral principles to some particular degree of heroism.

Molière rendered things with greater depth than the other poets; therefore, he was more moral. Nothing is simpler than this. Morality is in the essence of things. The more philosophical one is, the more easily one can see that virtue is the most likely road to happiness, that both in the palace and in the ordinary home, there can scarcely be happiness without justice. Every tyrannical father sometimes tells himself that two weeks after his death, his family will be happier. But these big questions make Thalia grimace.

As soon as you dogmatize on the stage—as soon as you insult a faction or argue about a controversial point—those members of your audience who have any intelligence imagine that you are challenging their vanity. Instead of laughing at the ridiculous traits of your characters or sympathizing with their misfortunes, they start looking for arguments contrary to your own. This is why any interjection of politics kills a literary work.

Molière is immoral. At these words, I can see the pedants smile at me with amusement. No, gentlemen, Molière is not immoral because he uses such expressions as "cuckolded husband" and "enema." [1] People used those expressions in his day, just as in the time of Shakespeare they believed in

[1] See, in Madame Campan, Louis XIV's reaction to this.

witches. The effects that these details can produce today are independent of the will of those great artists.

It is even less true that Molière is immoral because Harpagon's son lacks respect for his father, and says to him:

> I don't want your gifts.

A father like Harpagon deserved hearing such a thing; and the fear of hearing it is the only thing that can restrain an old man in his immoderate love of money.

Molière's immorality comes from a higher source. In the time of Madame d'Epinay and Madame Campan, there was an approved and tasteful manner of dying, marrying, going bankrupt, killing a rival, etc. The letters of Madame du Deffand testify to this. There was no act of human life, serious or frivolous, which was not imprisoned in advance, as it were, in the imitation of a model. And whosoever deviated from that model provoked *laughter* because he had degraded himself—because he had shown a sign of stupidity. This was called "being in bad taste." The suffering of General Lally was in *good taste*.[2]

It is through lack of the *model* and recourse to the *reasonable thing* that an intelligent Spaniard or Englishman arriving in France can be ridiculous. And I approve the idea of

[2] The letters of Horace Walpole to Madame du Deffand on the subject of General Lally. In her letter of January 11, 1769, to Walpole (Vol. I, pp. 31–32), Madame du Deffand expressed herself on the death of Lally, and the moments which had preceded it, with a frivolousness which was truly atrocious. In his reply, Walpole gave vent to a strong indignation. One finds him saying the following:
"Ah, Madame, what horrors you have told me about! Let it never be said that the English are callous and ferocious. In truth, it is the French who have these qualities. Yes, yes. You are savages, you are Iroquois, you French. It is true that people have been massacred in England. But has anyone ever seen us clap our hands while watching the execution of a poor unfortunate—a general officer who had languished in prison for two years? . . . Good Heavens! I am most glad that I left Paris before that horrible scene! I should have got myself torn to pieces or put into the Bastille."
Cf. the *Mémoires* of Madame de Genlis.

ridiculing such a person. It may be owing to his superior intelligence that the newcomer departs from the accepted usages. But until more information is available, society is justified in assuming that it is owing to ignorance. (And one must be careful: an ignorance of little usages instantly proves inferiority of rank—a thing abhorred among the aristocracy.) Or again, it may be owing to stupidity. In any case, if the new arrival deserves to be made an exception because of his intelligence, let him demonstrate his wit by defending himself against our criticism. That will amuse us.

In 1780, when a musketeer came at six o'clock in the morning and pounded on the door of an investigation counselor to take him away in a hackney coach, people would say that evening, in relating the details of the raid, "The musketeer's behavior was very correct," or else, "He behaved very incorrectly." Depending upon this decision of society, the musketeer would be made a captain of cavalry two months later or would expect some other promotion.

Fidelity to the accepted model, but a flexible fidelity that could, when necessary, give evidence of some wit—such was the way of avoiding ridicule in a court; and our fathers called it *polite manners*. Hence the phrases: "That is the accepted thing to do," "That isn't done," and "That doesn't resemble anything in the world," which are so frequent in the French language.

In doing things considered ridiculous, one loses *esteem*. Now at the court of Louis XIV (where real merit scarcely counted), to lose esteem was to lose one's worldly position entirely. When an important appointment came up a month after a vacancy, the *public opinion* of the court declared that it was either *ridiculous* or *proper* for Monsieur So-and-So to apply for it.

It is precisely this dread of not being like everybody else that inspires Molière, and that is why he is *immoral*.

To resist oppression—not to dread a danger because it is *hidden*—this is what may be called not being like everybody else. And yet this is the way one must be in our day in order to live happily or immune to attack from the local subprefect. Every timid man who dreads a danger because it is *hidden* will always find a subprefect to annoy him or a vicar-general to inform on him. In France, people with this sort of character have no refuge other than Paris, where they come and populate half of the new streets.

Under a king, fashionable taste allows of only one model and, if I may be permitted to treat fashionable taste as clothing, one *pattern*. Under a government like that of Washington, a hundred years from now, when idleness, vanity, and luxury will have replaced the Presbyterian melancholy, fashionable taste will allow of five or six accepted patterns instead of just one. In other words, it will tolerate much more originality among people. This will be true both in tragedy and in the choice of a buggy, in epic poetry and in the art of knotting a tie, because everything is to be found in human heads. The same penchant for pedantry that makes us give preference in painting to the art of drawing (which is scarcely anything more than an exact science) makes us adhere to the alexandrine and precise rules in drama, or to the instrumental symphony, roughly scraped and without soul, in music.

Molière fills one with a dread of not being like everybody else. One example of this is the way in which Ariste, the brother in *L'Ecole des Maris* who is a *raisonneur,* talks to Sganarelle, the eccentric brother, about fashion in clothes. Another example is Philinte preaching to Alceste, the misanthropist, on the art of living happily. The principle is always the same: be like everybody else.[3]

This tendency on the part of Molière was probably the political reason for his winning the king's favor. Louis XIV never forgot that when he was still young, the Fronde had forced him to leave Paris. Since the time of Caesar, men of power have hated eccentrics like Cassius who avoid popular pleasures and do as they like. The despot says to himself: "People like that might very well have courage. Moreover,

---

[3] A lady of my acquaintance, in order to keep herself occupied in the country, has attempted to draw up a course on morality based on the role of the *raisonneur* in Molière. This little work removes any doubts. I have not quoted it here, because it would be tedious, and I fear I have already gone beyond the scope of a literary pamphlet.

they attract attention and might very well, in case of need, become leaders of parties." Any notability not consecrated by itself is hateful to power.

Sterne was only too right: we are nothing but *well-rubbed coins*. But it is not time that has worn us down; it is the *dread of ridicule*. This is the true name for what the moralists often call *an excess of civilization, corruption,* etc. This is the fault of Molière. This is what kills moral courage in a people who are so brave when they have sword in hand. They dread a peril that might be ridiculous. The boldest man does not dare to yield to his hot-bloodedness except insofar as he is sure of walking in the approved path. But on the other hand, when hot-bloodedness (which is the opposite of vanity, the dominant passion) produces its effects, one sees the incredible and sublime follies of attacks on fortresses and the thing that is so terrifying to foreign soldiers under the name of *furia francese*.

It was obviously the chief business of Richelieu and Louis XIV to *smother moral courage.*[4]

A likable woman was saying to me this evening, in her salon: "Just look at how they abandon us. Here are seven of us women alone. All the men are over there around the card table or next to the fireplace talking politics." I said to myself: "Molière is responsible for some of this stupidity. Isn't this one of the results of *Les Femmes savantes?*"

Women are deathly afraid of the ridicule that Molière heaped on the pedantic Armande. And so instead of learning ideas, they learn music. Mothers do not at all fear the ridiculousness of having their daughters sing

Di piacer mi balza il cor

.   .   .

E l'amico che farà?

Gazza Ladra

because Molière did not name it publicly in *Les Femmes savantes.*

[4] The confessions of Agrippa d'Aubigné are like a novel by Sir Walter Scott. In them one sees how welcome hidden dangers still were in France about 1600.

According to this fine manner of reasoning, since the decline of the frivolous style (1788), women can only either love or hate; and in most cases they are incapable of discussing and understanding the reasons for loving and hating.

If, in the time of Madame Campan or the Duchess de Polignac the women were not *neglected,* it was because they understood very well—better, in fact, than anyone else—the things considered ridiculous at court. This is quite comprehensible, since they did them; and the opinion of the court was the equivalent of fortune.[5] The mental acuity of the women, their subtle tactfulness, and their passionate ardor to promote the worldly success of their gentlemen friends[6] made them admirable both in holding court and in depicting it.[7] Unfortunately, the objects of public attention have changed; and those women who have not kept up with events are in no position to understand the reasons which make a *protestation* ridiculous or abominable. They can only repeat, after the man they love: "It is hateful!" or "It is sublime." But when approbation is carried to such a point it is no longer flattering, but merely boring.

Many women in Paris are sufficiently happy if they can dress very carefully every evening, get into a carriage, and go to put in a half-hour appearance in a salon where the men talk among themselves on one side of the room while the women look one another over with a critical eye. In a society so arranged, a woman who did not have a sufficiently robust vanity to thrive exclusively on pleasures of this kind, would be most unhappy. In everything that makes up the pleasures

[5] The letters of Madame du Deffand to Horace Walpole.
[6] The *Mémoires* of Marmontel.
[7] It is in the letters of Madame de Sévigné, Madame de Caylus, Mademoiselle Aïssé, *et al.* that one should seek the *Age of Louis XIV.* Voltaire's *Siècle de Louis XIV* is puerile, somewhat like the *Révolution* of Madame de Staël. One is only too much aware that Voltaire would have traded all his genius for noble birth. Carried away by the elegance of its manners, Voltaire saw the *Age of Louis XIV* only in the embellishments of Paris and in the arts. It is very strange that a man of honor who had been caned with impunity by a *grand seigneur* should stubbornly continue to adore the political regime which had made him vulnerable to this little unpleasantness.

of the other women, she would find only emptiness. She would be considered odd. Society, which she would offend without knowing it because of her particular way of feeling things, would be judge in its own cause against her and would condemn her unanimously. I can visualize such a woman, after three years, with her reputation destroyed—while yet remaining the only one worthy of being loved. (True, one can interrupt the course of this malicious stupidity of the public by a six months' stay in the country.)

Since, unfortunately, the peoples of the world have been possessed by a mania for reasoning and a passion for constitutional rights, the chartist spirit, as it makes its way through Europe, will one day notice at its feet *the old rules of decorum* and will smash them with a flap of the wing. Then we shall see the end of that famous maxim, the palladium of our grandfathers' *savoir-vivre: One must be like everybody else.* Then, too, we shall see the decrepitude of Molière.

Love—a great, passionate love; or, failing that, familial sentiments based on a mutual tenderness for children—these are the strong bonds that attach us to women from our beginning in life. Rather annoyed by the egoism and deceits of men, whom we know only too well, we want to spend the last years of life quietly in the company of those who lent charm to its first moments and whose ever lively and sparkling imagination still recalls the most beautiful part of love.

Such is the manner of spending the last days of autumn in those happy lands where the despotism of *ridicule* (which, for more than is generally realized, is the ally and support of another despotism) has never been known; in those countries where amiable monarchy *à la* Philip II, not disguised by the falsehoods of courtiers feigning happiness, has not been able to deceive the people and has remained, with its hideous visage and frightful stare, exposed to all eyes. Because public education is only a mockery, all ideas are acquired by conversation; and the women have at least as much genius as the men. Because there has never been a court with unlimited power over public opinion, presided over by a despot jealous of superiority in any form, everyone has been free to seek happiness in his own way.

In Rome or Venice, a woman of superior intelligence is admired, feared, and adored; but no one entertains the idea of ruining her reputation by ridicule. It would be an absurd thing to attempt; and in those happy lands, the phrase I have employed would not even be understood. Because, in the last analysis, the salon of such a woman is the one where the greatest enjoyment is to be found, society grows accustomed to a few rather lively mistakes (if indeed she has to reproach herself with any) and always comes back to her in the end. Prudery is left in a corner, to yawn and disapprove. Consider the Roman princesses of the last century: for example, the one who saw to it that Pius VI received the tiara.[8] The great men of their day, who bore the names of Querini,[9] Consalvi, or Canova, found in those princesses confidantes for all their ideas, counselors for all their projects, and, finally, never that *moral inferiority* so frightful to discover in the person one loves.

I have no fear of some day seeming to be outmoded by mentioning a recent act of courage that occupies the thoughts of everyone in France.[10] "Well!" some young man will tell

[8] Madame Falconieri, a great lady much given to intrigue, who was considered to have a great deal of influence. She was the mother of the young lady who later became the Duchess di Braschi, through her marriage to one of the nephews of Pius VI. This pontiff was indebted to her for his first successes in his ecclesiastical career. But Madame Falconieri, who as a patroness was most valuable and had to be handled with great care, possessed none of those qualities that could make her loved as a mistress. Braschi kept company with her only for a short time and took his departure as soon as he had obtained the only favor he expected of her. It is only recently that the irritation he aroused in many respects, and his blind fondness for Mademoiselle Falconieri (who became his niece), have caused it to be said that he was her father. (*Mémoires historiques et philosophiques sur Pie VI*, Vol. I, p. 119.)

[9] The last great man of Venice.

[10] The resistance of M. Manuel, on March 4, 1832, to the decision of the day before, which barred him from the Chamber of Deputies.

you. "The woman I love has the kind of soul required to admire him, and with enthusiasm. All she lacks is the habit of a little attention and the logic needed to understand all the beauty of that magnanimous act, and all its consequences."

There is no doubt that Molière deserved well of Louis XIV in telling the women (represented by Bélise): "Beware of acquiring ideas."

> . . . Une femme en sait toujours assez
> Quand la capacité de son esprit se hausse
> A connaître un pourpoint d'avec un haut-de-chausse.

> (A woman always knows enough when the capacity of her mind is raised to the point where she can tell a doublet from a pair of breeches.)

Les Femmes savantes, Act II, Scene vii

It is by no means Louis XIV whom I blame: he was simply doing his job as king. (When will we do ours—we who are born with six thousand francs of private income?) The proof that Louis XIV saw things clearly is the fact that Madame Roland, a little *bourgeoise* of Paris, the daughter of a mere engraver, who was too poor to go to the theatre and had perhaps never seen *Les Femmes savantes,* was able with her penetrating mind to undo several great projects skillfully planned by the secret counselors of Louis XVI.

It is true, of course, that she had the stupidity to read in her youth. I recently witnessed a scolding given to a charming young girl, although she is only twelve years old, because she had dared to open a book that her mother was reading—the most proper book in the world. Whereupon the music teacher arrived and, in my presence, had the girl sing the duet from *L'Italiana in Algieri:*

> Ai capricci della sorte,

> .   .   .

> Sarà quel che sarà.

Act I

Amiable mother with your superior intelligence, books are like the lance of Achilles, which alone could heal the wounds it made. Teach your daughter the art of avoiding mistakes, if you want her to be able, some day, to resist the seductions of love, or those of hypocrisy at forty. In politics, as in the most private education, a bayonette can do nothing against a doctrine. At the very most, all it can do is cause a redoubling of attention to seize it. Books are multiplying so fast that your charming daughter will find the one you fear, even though it be in the cupboard of a country inn. And then you will see how that allegedly bad book will avenge itself for your past scoldings. It will be the book's turn to triumph and your turn to wear the ugly mien of an apprehended policeman. Some day, perhaps, you will be nothing more to your daughter than an envious woman who tried to deceive her. What a frightful image for a mother!

Molière tried to render impossible, by the success of *Les Femmes savantes,* the existence of women worthy of understanding and liking the misanthropist, Alceste. Madame Roland would have liked him.[11] And a man like this, supported by a woman worthy of understanding him, might have become a citizen-hero—a Hampden. Consider this danger, and remember that a despot is always afraid.

But, I am told, Molière did not give the slightest thought to all these Machiavellian depths. All he wanted was to make people laugh. But in this case, why say that Regnard is immoral and Molière is not?

The comedy, *Les Femmes savantes,* is a masterpiece, but an immoral masterpiece that resembles nothing in this world. A man of letters in our society is no longer a buffoon maintained by the *grands seigneurs.* He is a man who takes pleasure in thinking instead of working, and who is consequently without much money. Or else he is an agent of the police who is paid by the treasury to write pamphlets. Is this kind of person a Trissotin or a Vadius?[12]

[11] I use the name of Madame Roland to indicate to myself the names of women of *superior genius* who are still living.

[12] Characters in *Les Femmes savantes* with ridiculous literary pretensions. [Translator's note.]

Chapter 9

On the Morality of Regnard

FIFTY YEARS AGO, during the rather prim reign of Madame Dubarry or of Madame de Pompadour, to mention something immoral was to be immoral.

Beaumarchais depicted a guilty mother in all the horrors of remorse. If there is one spectacle in the world calculated to make us shudder, it is that of the poor Countess Almaviva at the knees of her husband. And this spectacle is seen every day by women who have probably never read a single sermon—not even Bourdaloue's sermon against *Tartuffe*. Still, Beaumarchais is immoral.

"Say rather that he is lacking in gaiety; that his comedy often elicits horror because the author did not have that sublime artistry which, in *Le Tartuffe*, tends constantly to diminish the odious."

"No, Beaumarchais is utterly improper."

"Well and good. We are too close to that man of wit to judge him. In a hundred years the Faubourg Saint-Germain will still not have had time enough to forgive him for the trick he played on the despotism of decorum, in 1784, when he had his delicious *Figaro* performed."

"Regnard is immoral," people say to me. "Just look at his *Légataire universel*."

To which I reply: "The Jesuits of Franche-Comté, established at Rome, would never have dared to risk the hoax of Crispin dictating the will of Géronte while the latter was lying in a stupor[1]—and that in the presence of a councilor of the *parlement* of Dijon and a canon from the same city—if they had had any grounds to fear that those gentlemen had,

[1] Cf. *Le Légataire universel,* Act IV, Scene vi. Stendhal here apparently refers to a similar hoax allegedly perpetrated by the Jesuits in question. [Translator's note.]

70

even once in their lives, seen a performance of Regnard's *Légataire*.

What is sublime in the talent of that likable man, who lacked both genius and a passion for literary fame, is the fact that he makes us laugh while witnessing such an invidious act. The only lesson that comedy can give us—*a warning to dupes* and ridiculous persons—is given. And yet this lofty lesson has not cost us a single moment of boredom or a single impulse of impotent rage. This is more than one can say of *Le Tartuffe*. I can no longer see that masterpiece without thinking of the town of Saint-Quentin-sur-Isère and a certain *Réponse aux lettres anonymes*.[2]

As far as the *manner of portrayal* is concerned, it seems to me that *Le Légataire universel* represents perfection in comedy. The English give us a *Beverley* who kills himself. This amounts to showing me, in a spiritual manner, one of the shortcomings of this melancholy life with which a blind Providence endowed us in a moment of distraction. I have no need of such a picture of life. I know only too well that life is not a primrose path. The good Lord deliver us from dramas and dramaturgists! And, along with them, from all feelings of hate or indignation! I find only too much of it in the newspapers. Instead of the gloomy, dull Beverley, Regnard gives us the brilliant Valère,[3] who, first of all, knowing that he is a *gambler*, does not marry. This is virtue—and exactly as much of it as can be put into comedy.

If he were to kill himself, he would do it gaily, without thinking of it any longer than the time required to load a

---

[2] An allusion to the crime of Father Maingrat, the parish priest of Saint-Quentin, Département of Isère. See the pamphlet entitled *Réponse aux anonymes qui ont écrit des lettres à Paul-Louis Courier, vigneron*, No. 2, dated from Veretz, February 6, 1823.

Here is an immoral trend, O men of power! Since you have the effrontery to speak of immorality, think of thirty thousand young people waiting, in the last rays of the sunset on a beautiful evening in spring . . . in a box, in the depths of that solitary church. "Box"=confessional. [Translator's note.]

[3] The leading character in Regnard's play, *Le Joueur*. [Translator's note.]

pistol. But no. A man like Valère has enough *moral courage* to go off to Greece in search of emotions and to get into the war agaist the Turks when he has no more than five hundred *louis* left.

The amiable Regnard, knowing very well that the human heart never entertains more than one true passion at a time, puts the following words into the mouth of Valère, who has been abandoned by a mistress for whom he grieves:

> . . . Et le jeu, quelque jour,
> Saura bien m'acquitter des pertes de l'amour.

(And gambling, some day, will recompense me for my losses in love.) /

This is true comedy. Except for the matter of genius, this is better stuff than sending the poor misanthropist to die of desolation and bad humor in his Gothic chateau, deep in the provinces. It is the subject of *Le Joueur*. The first, so essentially gloomy, ends on a gay note. The comedy of the misanthropist, which could be very funny because it involves only ridiculous traits, has a gloomy ending. Here we have the difference in the tendency of the two authors. Here we have the difference between true comedy, intended to cheer the spirits of busy people, and that comedy which was intended to amuse people *who were malicious and had no other occupation than backbiting.* Such were the courtiers of Louis XIV.

We are of greater worth than our ancestors, and we are less given to hatred than they were. Why should we be treated like them? [4]

Alceste was only a poor *républicain* who lived in the wrong time and place. If people had known geography in the time of Molière, Philinte would have said to his friend: "Leave for the young and growing city of Philadelphia." That churlish genius was ready-made for republicanism. He would

---

[4] See the France of 1620 in the first volume of Basompierre's *Mémoires.* It takes a hundred years for political changes to be translated into manners and morals. Consider the gloomy melancholy of Boston.

have joined a Puritan church in New York, and been received like Gribourdon in Hell.[5]

I believe that there is more happiness for people in Washington; but it is a coarse kind of happiness, a bit uncouth, and scarcely suitable for one who holds a yearly ticket to the *opera buffa*. There is probably a great deal of *good sense* there; but the people laugh less than they do in Paris —even the Paris of today, which for seven or eight years has been imprisoned [poisoned?] by the hatreds between the Faubourg Saint-Germain and the Chaussée-d'Antin.

Consider the lampoons attempted during the past two months (March, 1823) against a cabinet minister, M. de Villèle, whose position is coveted by others. In Washington, they would have attacked this minister with arguments of a mathematical demonstrability. But still the minister would not have been ousted. The only difference is that we would not have laughed. Over there, the government is merely a banking house paid, at reduced rates, for providing one with justice and personal safety. But, at the same time, a knavish government does not educate people who remain a bit uncouth and barbarous. I have a high regard for our small provincial manufacturers; and virtue is to be found in the class of small landowners with a hundred *louis* of income from their properties. But if I were invited to spend four hours at one of their dinners, I would yawn with boredom.

Laughter is a trait of our monarchical and corrupt manners and morals that I would very much dislike to lose. I am aware that this is not too reasonable a thing to say. But what can I do? I was born French; I would rather suffer an injustice than be bored for six months; and when I am with uncivilized people I don't know what to say. A *republic* is the contrary of *laughter*. This is why I console myself for living today rather than a hundred years from now. Men of republican spirit are ceaselessly engaged in their business affairs with an exaggerated degree of seriousness. There are always a few Wilkeses[6] to start them trembling about the

---

[5] I.e., very well. Cf. Voltaire, *La Pucelle,* Chant V. [Translator's note.]
[6] One of the champions of political liberty in England. Born in London in 1727; died in 1797.

imminent danger to their country, which is going to perish in three months. Now any man who is concerned—I will not say impassioned, but merely seriously concerned—with some thing or some interest, is incapable of *laughing*. He has other things to do than *idly* to compare himself to his neighbor.

The Regnards of this world have a need of insouciance. This is why there are so few comedies in Italy, the land of love and hatred. Rossini, when he is good, makes me dream of my mistress. M. Argan, the *Malade imaginaire,* makes me laugh (in those moments when there is a coarse streak in my soul) at the expense of that sad thing, humanity. This latter type of ridicule is proper to men of republican spirit.

What will become of that young man of twenty who came this morning to borrow my copy of Malthus, and whom I can see making his début in a political career—even a virtuous one? He will spend ten years in political discussions of the just and the unjust, the legal and the illegal.

Should I give more approval to the wise philosopher who, having withdrawn from social life because of his weak chest, is spending his life finding new reasons for holding both himself and the rest of humanity in contempt? A person of this kind cannot laugh. What does he see in Falstaff's charming account, to Prince Henry, of a nocturnal brawl? Just one more misery for poor human nature—a vapid lie prompted by a base pecuniary interest. Once arrived at this viewpoint, a person sees things clearly, if you will. But such a person is no longer good for anything but adorning the wardens' pew in a Puritan church or, like Bentham, writing a commentary on the Criminal Code.

"But," an alarmed laugher will say to me, "in losing the court, did we lose everything that is ridiculous? And shall we no longer laugh because there is no more Oeil-de-Boeuf?"

First of all, it is quite possible that we shall get the Oeil-de-Boeuf back again: people are laboring hard toward this end. In the second place, happily, and fortunately for the cause of laughter, we have merely *displaced* the object of our cult. Instead of being at Versailles, it is on the boulevard. In Paris, the *fashionable thing* has replaced the *court*.

Last evening I was saying to a little man of eight years and a half, "My friend Edmond, do you want me to send you some meringue cakes tomorrow?

"Yes, if they are from Félix's.[7] They are the only ones I like. The others have a detestable taste. . . ."

I gave my friend a hug and took him on my knee. He was completely absurd. I behaved like a *grande dame* with Rousseau: I wanted to examine this ridiculous trait of his more closely. Looking him over, I noticed that he was dressed in a long blue cloak with a leather belt. "So you are dressed as a Cossack?" I asked him.

"No, Monsieur, I am dressed as a Gaul." And I noticed that his mother, a pretty, serious woman of twenty-five, was looking at me askance because I had been clumsy enough not to recognize the Gaulish costume. Because of course *one must* be in Gaulish costume.

How is it to be expected that my little friend, when he reaches the age of twenty, will think of anything else in the world besides his spurs and his forbidding, military bearing when he enters a café? No, I am not worried about the younger generation: there will be no lack of ridiculous traits among them. Nor will there be any lack of comedy, if we can manage to get rid of censorship and Laharpe. The former can be done very quickly; but acquiring good taste is something that takes much longer: it will probably require three hundred pamphlets and six thousand literary articles signed Dussault.

Molière knew as much as, and even more than, Regnard about extracting the most odious things from the comical. But the *decorum* that Louis XIV had introduced into manners ran counter to an appreciation of this genre. In order to ridicule doctors, one must show them prescribing remedies *ab hoc et ab hac* for their patients. But this comes close to the role of the murderer. It is something odious; it makes people indignant; and hence there is no more laughter. What can be done? One takes a *bon vivant*, the most insouciant of men and hence the farthest removed, in our eyes, from the role of murderer and gives him, against his will, the role

[7] A pastry baker in the Passage des Panoramas.

of doctor. This person will be obliged to prescribe remedies haphazardly. The other characters will take him to be a real doctor, and he will look exactly like one. From then on, for a mischievous and witty people, it will be impossible to see a real doctor at the bedside of a young lady without recalling, by means of a humorous saying, Sganarelle prescribing a dose of "purgative escape with two drams of matrimonium in the form of pills."[8] The poet's end will have been accomplished: the doctors have a ridiculous trait, and the clever absurdity of the plot has saved us from black horror.

I open the three volumes in which they have given us the *Mémoires* of Madame de Campan.

> During the first half of the reign of Louis XV, the ladies still wore the *court apparel of Marly,* so designated by Louis XIV, which differed but little from that adopted for Versailles. The *robe française,* pleated in the back, with big hoop petticoats, replaced the former attire, and was retained, at Marly, until the end of the reign of Louis XVI. The diamonds, feathers, rouge, and embroidered or gold-lamé fabrics dissipated the least appearance of a country sojourn.

(I have the feeling that I am reading a description of a Chinese court.)

> After dinner and before the time set for games of cards, the queen, the princesses, and their ladies in waiting, driven by servants wearing the king's livery, in *carrioles* with canopies richly embroidered in gold, went through the groves of Marly where the trees, which had been planted by Louis XIV, were of a prodigious height.

This last line was written by Madame Campan. It is hardly likely that it would have come from the pen of a writer of the age of Louis XIV. The latter would have thought of some detail in the embroidery on the canopies of the *carrioles* rather than the tall, thickly-foliaged trees and their shade. Such things had no charm for the *grands seigneurs*

---

[8] *Le Médecin malgré lui,* Act III, Scene vi.

who, during a whole century, came to live in the country among the trees.

In addition to the sentimental style that lends such a glitter to *Le Rénégat* [9] and *Le Génie du Christianisme*, we have genuine feeling. The French public has only recently discovered the beauties of nature. They were still almost entirely unknown to Voltaire. Rousseau made them fashionable by exaggerating them with his usual rhetoric. One finds the true feeling for them in Sir Walter Scott, although his descriptions often strike me as overly long, especially when they come in the middle of a passionate scene. Shakespeare used descriptions of the beauties of nature in just proportions: Mark Antony, in his speech to the Roman people over the body of Caesar; and Banquo in his reflection on the site of Macbeth's castle and the martlets that like to nest there.

Because in the time of Molière the beauties of nature had not yet been discovered, a feeling for them is often lacking in his works. This gives them a certain dryness. It is like the effect in the paintings of Raphael's early period, before Fra Bartolomeo had taught him the art of chiaroscuro. Molière was better endowed than other men for depicting the frailty of the human heart. He was hopelessly enamored and jealous and said of the woman he loved: "I cannot blame her if she feels the same irresistible urge to be a coquette that I feel to love her."

It is a beautiful spectacle, and very consoling for us, to see extreme philosophy vanquished by love. But art did not yet dare to depict such a nature. Racine would have depicted it; but because he was encumbered by the alexandrine line, like a knight of the old days in his armor, he was unable to render precisely those nuances of the heart that he perceived better than others. Love, that passion which is so visionary, demands in its language a mathematical exactness. It cannot make do with a kind of diction that always says either too much or too little (and which always recoils before the right word).

Another cause of the feeling of dryness in the comedies of Molière is the fact that in his time people were only just

[9] The title of a novel by M. le vicomte d'Arlincourt.

beginning to pay attention to emotions of some subtlety. Molière could never have written *Les Fausses confidences* or *Le Jeu de l'amour et du hasard* of Marivaux—plays that we censure hypocritically, but which give all young people the delicious sensation of hearing themselves told "I love you!" by the pretty lips of Mademoiselle Mars.

Molière has difficulty using the alexandrine line. He often says too much or too little, or else he uses an ornate style which is ridiculous today. In France it is the *natural* which never becomes ridiculous as it grows older. Pomposity is contrary to the genius of the language. I see in the example of Balzac[10] the fate that awaits MM. de Chateaubriand, Marchangy, d'Arlincourt, and their school.

[10] Member of the Académie Française. Born in 1594, died in 1655.

Chapter 10

Luther, by Werner[1]

(A play closer to the masterpieces of Shakespeare than are the tragedies of Schiller.)

IF I WERE AIMING at a kind of trivial cautiousness, I would
not advise you to read the first four acts of *Luther*.[2] I would
not say—quite bluntly, and in a way that invites the mockery
of the classical rhymers: It is in Werner's masterpiece that
you will find an accurate portrayal of Germany in the fifteenth
century and of that great revolution which changed the face of
Europe. That revolution also told the nations: "Examine
before believing. And it is precisely because a man is be-
decked in crimson that you should beware of him." It is
plain to see that that revolution, in its means and its phases,
was similar to the revolution of today. The struggle between
the kings and the common people was already going on.

Instead of wearying yourself by seeking for that impos-
ing spectacle in huge tomes, which are conducive to boredom, go to the theatre of Berlin and see *Luther*, a romantic
tragedy. In three hours you will not only get to know the
fifteenth century, but, knowing it because you have seen
it in action, you will never be able to forget it. And for us,
who have scarcely reached the midway point in the revolution of the nineteenth century, it means a great deal to see,
in three hours, the entire development of the revolution of the
fifteenth century, which was absolutely similar. For "liberal
principle" read "Luther," and the resemblance is identical.
You will never forget the great spectacle provided by the
Emperor Charles V judging Luther at the Diet of Worms.
You will be deeply moved. It has now been fifteen years since

[1] Friedrich Ludwig Zacharias Werner, German dramatist (1768–
1823). [Translator's note.]
[2] In the excellent translation made by the respectable M. Michel
Berr, which forms a part of the collection of the *Théâtres étrangers,* published by the bookseller, Ladvocat, Vol. XVII.

I last saw *Luther* performed, but I can still visualize that other scene so sublime in its simplicity: Luther welcoming his father and mother, who, troubled in their old age by both the good and the evil being said of their son, undertook despite their advanced years a long trip of a hundred leagues to see again the son who had left them, twenty years before, as an impoverished student. The combination of the naïveté of the son recalling to his father the latter's too-strict punishments, and the great man telling him of his life and the battles he has to fight, forms a sublime spectacle, in my opinion. The gentle Melanchthon, the Fénelon of the Reformation, is present during this simple conversation. Luther explains his new doctrines to his father, a Saxon miner. To make himself understood, he uses analogies drawn from the work of miners. He tries to be as simple as possible. In this way the reader understands the essence of the things for which he is going to see Luther persecuted. In the middle of this talk, which makes Luther's aged mother tremble at the account of the dangers that he has not altogether succeeded in concealing, he suddenly stops short. He is afraid of being carried away by the demon of pride.

Luther is not weary of his mission. Rather, he *doubts*. This is the trait of genius whose light illumines the entirety of Werner's tragedy. This doubt shows us immediately that Luther is a person of complete sincerity. And what man was better equipped to depict in Luther all the nuances of doubt than Werner, who, after having been an ardent Protestant and unjust toward the Catholics, only recently died in Vienna (in 1823) as a Catholic priest, a sublime preacher in his new religion, and finally, to make the whole thing complete, a Jesuit? He had left the Jesuit monastic life—still intolerant, impassioned, unjust toward his adversaries, and by the same token both a good Jesuit and a great poet. Not a great poet only because of his beautiful poetry, but a great poet because his impetuous behavior demonstrated the fact to all men. And in my opinion he was a greater poet than Schiller. Although Schiller wrote better lines, he had inherited from the dramas of Racine the practice of having his characters question and answer one another in tirades of eighty lines. There is none of this boredom in Werner's masterpiece. And yet what subject would lend itself better to the tirade than that of an impassioned fanatic converting his fellow countrymen by preaching? But Werner was a man of intelligence.

I come back to that special quality of this tragedy about Luther: one can never forget it. If we had seen the great events in the history of France in the same way, instead of hesitating and being obliged to open Lesage's historical atlas from time to time, all our national catastrophes would be etched in blood on our memories. The expression "etched in blood" warns us of the great obstacle that romanticism will have to face. Our annals are so loathsomely bloody, our best kings have been so barbarous, that our history will at every moment be difficult to present with candor. How does one show Francis I ordering the burning of Dolet, who passed for his natural son, because the latter was suspected of heresy? What French king would permit this disparagement of his predecessors and, by the same token, of the authority he has inherited from them? [3] It is much better to hide the whole thing under the pomposity of the alexandrine. A man whose face has been hideously marred by congenital blemishes requires a helmet and a lowered visor. This is why the kings will encourage their academies to heap abuse upon the romantics.

The latter were supposed to make concessions, employ tact, tell only a part of the truth, and above all spare the vanity of little men still alive. All these things no doubt help one to be successful. But to do this would mean being a classicist, while preaching romanticism. All these precautions and quasi-falsehoods were in style forty years ago. Today, after the *Holy Alliance,* no one can deceive anyone else. Distrust, implanted in the hearts of all by more important pursuits, will extend its influence even to games of literature. We have to play with our cards on the table now. And if anyone

[3] Philip II sends the Duke of Alba to conquer Holland . . . The town of Naarden refuses to surrender. The duke assembles his troops under the walls of the unfortunate town; it requests capitulation . . . this deed is horrible. For reasons of deference, I have omitted a very similar incident from the history of Catherine de' Medici. (Watson, Book XII.)

hides them, the press is there to expose the truth—and the public to accord only its contempt to whosoever has once tried to deceive it.

I am setting forth in clear and imprudent terms what seems to me to be the truth. If I am mistaken, the public will soon have forgotten me. But whatever abuses the classicists may heap upon me, I am safe from contempt, because I have been frank. At the very most, it will perhaps be said that I attach too much importance to all this. An hour from now, I myself will laugh at the sentence I have just written: it betrays the man who has just reread *Luther* with enthusiasm. But I probably will not delete that sentence. It seemed true to me when I wrote it; and the man excited by the spectacle of a great action is at least the equal of an *homme de salon* recalled to strict prudence by the sight of cold-hearted people. *Luther* is perhaps the best play since Shakespeare.

I would have liked to see a scene giving some idea of the opposition party: an Italian monk selling indulgences and then, with his receipts for the day, paying a prostitute in a cabaret and coming to blows with another monk.

The kind and gentle seriousness of the German, whose thought gets lost in the clouds, is struck by this spectacle, which largely accounts for the strength of Luther.

Chapter 11

A Reply to Some Objections[1]

1.

PLATO HAD THE SOUL OF A POET, and Condillac the soul of a surgeon-anatomist. The ardent and tender soul of Plato felt things which will forever be beyond the ken of Condillac and those like him.

A few years ago there was a bad male dancer at the *Opéra* who was at the same time a very distinguished engraver. It would hardly have been proper for him to say to those who reproached him for dancing badly: "Just look at how well I do engraving. And is not engraving a much more noble art than the dance?"

Such was Plato: an impassioned soul, a sublime poet, a captivating poet, a writer of the first rank—and a puerile reasoner. See, for example, in the translation by M. Cousin, the quaint arguments advanced by Socrates (*inter alia*, p. 169, Vol. I).

Ideology[2] is not only a tedious science but an impertinent one. It is as though a man stopped you in the street and proposed to teach you how to walk. To which you would reply: "Haven't I been walking for twenty years, and don't I walk very well?" But it is nonetheless true that three-fourths of mankind walk badly and in such a way that they tire quickly. The people who would reject this impertinent proposal the most sharply are those who walk the best and who have invented on their own an imperfect art of walking well.

---

[1] This chapter constitutes for the most part a reply to a letter written by the poet, Lamartine, after reading the first part (Chapters I–III) of *Racine and Shakespeare,* to one Mareste, an acquaintance of Stendhal. For the text of the letter, see Appendix [Translator's note.]

[2] I.e., the theory that all ideas derive from sensations. Condillac was a leading proponent of this theory. [Translator's note.]

It is pleasant to believe that one learns ideology in reading a great poet like Plato, who is sometimes obscure, but with the kind of obscurity which lofty souls find moving and enticing. By contrast, there is nothing so dry and discouraging as the writings of Condillac. Because he claims to see things clearly, but does not see the noble and generous aspects of life, he seems to condemn it to a state of nothingness. Because we feel that he sees very clearly. These are two of the reasons why many people destined by nature for the arts, but lazy like all of us, get lost in the clouds[3] with the divine Plato as soon as they try to reason about things which are a bit lofty and difficult. If they are challenged on this point, they very quickly grow angry and say to their attacker: "You have a soul which is cold, arid, and common." To which one might reply: "At least I'm not lazy. And I have taken the trouble to learn ideology from the philosophers and not from the poets."

If there is any story which has been rehashed time and again in the books, it is the following. Voltaire had consented to hear some lines of poetry read by a young lady who aspired to a career in the theatre. She began with some lines from the role of Aménaïde. The great man, astounded by her lack of warmth, asked her: "But, Mademoiselle, if your lover had betrayed you and basely abandoned you, what would you do?" "I'd find another one," the girl replied ingenuously.

There you have the good sense of Condillac, as opposed to the genius of Plato. I will readily agree that in nineteen out of twenty cases, in the ordinary business of life, it is better to be reasonable and have good sense like that prudent young lady. The trouble comes when people of this kind want to get involved in the fine arts: to reason about them or, what is worse, to practice them. Just look at the example of the French musicians. The passions and the arts are merely a ridiculous importance attached to some little thing.

[3] J.-J. Rousseau, on the first page of *Emile*.

2.

"*Ideal beauty* is the first aim of the arts, but you do not say so." This is the second objection raised against me. My reply is: I thought we all agreed on this.

3.

I have two more things to say about *the beautiful*.

The first is that although I have much admiration for those painters who create *ideal beauty*, like Raphael and Correggio, I am by no means contemptuous of the painters I would willingly call *mirror painters*—those who, like Gaspard Poussin, reproduce nature exactly, as a mirror would. As I write this I can still see, after five years, the big landscapes of Gaspard that adorn the rooms of the Palazzo Doria at Rome and reproduce so well the sublime countryside around Rome. It is the merit of a good many Dutch painters that they have reproduced nature exactly and artlessly, like a mirror, and it is no small merit. It is especially delicious in landscapes, I think. You feel yourself suddenly plunged into a deep revery, of the kind evoked by the sight of the woods and *their vast silence*. You think deeply of your most cherished illusions. You find them less improbable; and soon they gladden you as if they were realities. You speak to the one you love. You dare to question her, and you hear what she says in reply. These are the feelings awakened in me when I walk alone in a real forest.

These mirror painters, in all the genres, are infinitely preferable to the vulgar persons who try to imitate Raphael. If such persons were capable of producing any effect at all, it would be to make one dislike Raphael. Likewise, Dorat, Destouches . . . have tried to write comedies like those of Molière. I much prefer the simple Carmontelle or Goldoni, who were *mirrors of nature*. Nature possesses strange aspects and sublime contrasts. They may remain unknown to the *mirror* which reproduces them without being aware of it.

What does it matter, so long as I experience their poignant pleasures?

This is my explanation for the charm of the oldest painters of the Italian schools: Bonifazio, Ghirlandajo, Mantegna, Masaccio, *et al.*

I prefer an old play of Massinger to Addison's *Cato*. I prefer Machiavelli's *Mandragora* to the comedies of that lawyer from Turin, M. Nota.

The man who describes his emotions is usually ridiculous. Because if that emotion has brought him happiness, and he does not speak in such a way as to reproduce that emotion[4] in those who are listening to him, he will arouse envy. And the more he has to do with vulgar people, the more ridiculous he will be.

One exception to this is terror. We never feel a repulsion for people who tell us ghost stories, however commonplace and vulgar they may be. All of us have known fear in our lives.

4.

Artists in the solemn genre are likely to feel disdain (which is also an attitude of stupidity) toward those artists whose aim is to make people *laugh*. The solemn ones enjoy an unjust privilege for which they are indebted to pure chance; and I can hardly see any loftiness in this. Let us refer it to the ignoble course of ambition. In the arts there must be greater nobility of soul, or one remains dull.

In that admirable novel, *Tom Jones,* the man of the people who is taken to a play felt that it was the king who gave the best performance in the tragedy. He is indignant when anyone dares to compare another character to the king, who, first of all, wore the best clothes and, in the second place, shouted the loudest. The common people—even those who travel in carriages—reproduce every day that fine sentiment they call a rational judgment. They scowl at everything that is not terribly noble. It is from this privileged class, destined by nature to be passionately fond of stuffed turkey and big

[4] Like J.-J. Rousseau in *Les Confessions.*

honorary ribbons, that we get the most vehement abuse of our poor Shakespeare.

The solemn artists tend to confuse, in all good faith, the *comical* and the *ugly;* i.e., things intentionally made faulty in order to provoke laughter, like Sancho Panza's manner of reasoning, are confused with things which are out-and-out ugly because they fail to be beautiful—things produced by a solemn artist who is trying for beauty and goes astray. An example of this is the sculptor who did the statue of Louis XIV naked, like Hercules, at the Porte-Saint-Denis and who, faithful to the periwig, like M. Bosio, let the king keep on his head a great, puffy periwig worth a thousand *écus*.

i have found this injustice toward *laughter* in Canova.[5] Among the great artists whom I have had the good fortune to approach, Vigano is the only one who has avoided this stupidity.

Do we demand that sculpture render movement? Or that the art of the Davids and the Girodets represent a perfect night? It would be equally absurd to demand of an artist that he *feel* the merit of another artist who is gaining immortality in the genre immediately bordering upon his own. If he found that genre preferable, he would work in it.

After having explained this idea to Canova as well as I could, in bad Italian, I said to him: "Do you want to lower yourself—you, a great man, who in your youth were so moved by the form of a cloud seen at midnight, when you were coming home, that you cried tears of joy—do you want to lower yourself to the crassitude of that banker (M. Torlonia, the Duke of Bracciano) who has accumulated ten millions through twenty-five years of arithmetic and some sordid ideas? In his box at the Teatro di Argentina, he thinks only of how to attack the impresario and pay him ten sequins less. He loudly condemns Cimarosa's musical inventions on the word *felicità* as lacking in dignity, and learnedly prefers the noble and solemn music of the Mayers and the Paers. But that music is boring! No matter. It is respectable.

"Admit quite frankly," I said to Canova, "and as it befits

5 Antonio Canova, Italian sculptor; born 1757, died 1822, at Venice. [Translator's note.]

the great man you are, that *non omnia possumus omnes;* that no matter how good our eyes may be, we cannot see both sides of an orange at once.

"You, the sublime creator of the *Three Graces* and the *Maddalena,* love only the noble and moving aspects of nature. They are the only ones which induce in you that gentle revery which constituted the happiness of your youth, on the lagoon at Venice, and the glory of your life. If you were to see the comical side of things first, you would no longer be yourself. For you, comedy is of value only as a means of entertainment.

"Then why do you hold forth on the subject of comedy? Why do you presume to dictate laws for a genre which you appreciate only in a secondary manner? Do you absolutely insist upon being universal? Leave that presumption to the poor devils who are not even particular.

"Have you deigned to notice how the common herd of people acquire a knowledge of the men of genius? When a hundred years have passed, and they see that no one has approached Milton, whom they held in great contempt while he was alive, they proclaim him a great poet. And they immediately explain his genius with some absurd reason.

"This is what is called the arithmetical method of appreciating beauty. Is it fit for you? The biographers lie learnedly when they show you great men honored during their lifetime. The common herd honors only generals of armies. For three-fourths of the inhabitants of Paris, before November 18, 1659,[6] Molière was nothing more than a buffoon. He was not even a member of the Academy—a position obtainable immediately by the least important abbé serving as tutor to the least important duke."

A boorish tax collector with the rank of *receveur général,* who no longer talks about anything but horses and landaus, seeing that in the past hundred years nothing so good as Scarron's *Roman comique* has appeared, will perhaps deign to close his eyes to the triviality of the role of Ragotin (he

[6] Date of the first performance of *Les Précieuses ridicules* at the Théâtre du Petit-Bourbon.

who for thirty years has curried favor with men like Ragotin!) and buy the works of Scarron, provided they are printed by Didot, on gilt-edged paper, and bound by Thouvenin.

A certain man of taste will immediately admire the noble *Clarissa Harlowe* or the works of Madame Cottin. But lend an ear to the conversation of people who never think of priding themselves on the literature they know, and you will hear the *Roman comique* quoted ten times for every one time for the noble Malek-Adel. This is because Ragotin has the *ideal beauty* of laughter. He is cowardly; he is vain; and he wants to please the women, though no taller than a boot. But, for all these fine qualities, we do not despise him absolutely; and this is why we laugh at him.

I regret the preceding sentences. For me there is nothing so respectable as a *ridiculous trait.* In the state of arid melancholy of a society patterned after the most severe vanity, a ridiculous trait, among all things in the world, is the one we should cultivate with the greatest assiduity in our friends. It makes us laugh to ourselves once in a while.

As for the men whom I honor, I am vexed at seeing them deny me the merit of Pigault-Lebrun, whereas a much inferior talent, provided it be in the *solemn style,* immediately elicits their praise. For example, *Jacques Fauvel,* where the women never dare to praise the comic element—and, especially, to discuss it in detail, as they discuss in detail the serious talent of Sir Walter Scott.

5.

The tender and overexcited souls who have been too lazy to seek out *ideology* in the philosophers and vain enough to believe that they learned it from Plato, are subject to another error. They say that there is an *absolute ideal beauty;* that, for example, if it had been given to Raphael and Titian to perfect themselves more at every instant, they would some day have produced *identically* the same pictures.

They forget that Raphael felt that what was most beautiful

in the looks of a young woman he met at the Colosseum was the *contour,* whereas Titian admired the *complexion* above everything else.

> No primrose path leads to glory,

La Fontaine said. Why isn't he still alive, so that he could repeat it, in every key, to the amiable but indolent persons I am attacking! These tender, overexcited, eloquent souls—the only ones in the world that I love—despise anatomy as an apothecary's science. Nonetheless, it is in the amphitheatre of the Jardin des Plantes, and nowhere else, that they will find the refutation of Plato's system regarding the identity of ideal beauty in all men. Voltaire said it in a style that I dare not employ, since refinement has made so much progress!

"For a toad, there is nothing more beautiful than his female toad, with her big eyes bulging out of her head."

Do people really believe, in good faith, that a brave Negro general from the island of Santo Domingo greatly admires the fresh complexions of the Maddalenas of Guido Reni?

People have different temperaments. The gloomy and impetuous Bossuet could never feel the charming and tender gentleness of Fénelon.

You may elevate as much as you like, in your thought, the faculties of these two great writers. You may imagine them constantly drawing closer to perfection. But still Bossuet will cry out, in a thunderous voice: "Madame is dying! Madame is dead!" And Fénelon will still say:

> Then Idoménée confessed to Mentor that he had never felt such a deeply moving pleasure as that of being loved, and of making so many people happy. "I never would have believed it," he said. "It seemed to me that all the glory of kings consisted only in making themselves feared, that the rest of mankind was made for them; and everything I had heard about kings who had been the love and delight of their subjects seemed a pure fable. Now I see the truth of it. But I must tell you how my heart was poisoned, from the time of my earliest childhood, as to the authority of

90

kings. This is the thing which has caused all the woes in my life." (Book XIII.)

Instead of becoming similar and drawing closer to each other, they constantly diverge. If they still resemble each other a little bit, it is because of shyness. It is because they do not dare write everything that their ardent souls suggest to them.

I dare not take the reader to the amphitheatre at the Jardin des Plantes. And it would perhaps be indiscreet to suggest that he then make a little trip to Saxony, followed by a two months' journey in Calabria. If, however, he were willing to study literature in this way, instead of reading, every two years, in the writings of the *philosopher in vogue,* a new explanation of *beauty,* he would soon conclude, on the basis of a thousand observed facts, that there are a great variety of temperaments and that there is no greater difference than that between a phlegmatic inhabitant of Dresden and an ill-tempered rogue of Cosenza.

At this point I would tell him—or rather, he would tell himself, which is much better—that the *ideal beauty* of such people differs. And six months or a year later he would finally arrive at the following enormous proposition that strikes him as so bizarre today.

Every human being, if he thought about it very hard, would have a different *ideal beauty*.

There are as many *ideal beauties* as there are different noses or different characters.

Mozart, who was born at Salzburg, did his work for phlegmatic, tender, and melancholy souls like himself; Cimarosa, for ardent and impassioned souls, who knew no respite from their passions, and never saw but one goal.

Persons of the most acute intelligence have denied these truths of mine. What must I conclude? That they are lacking in genius? That they have not written sublime works a thousand times superior to this pamphlet?

Such stupidity is the farthest thing from my mind. I shall conclude from this that they were lazy in their youth, or else that, once arrived at the age of forty, they have closed the door to new ideas.

Their children, who will have been reared after 1815, when these ideas are common,[7] will get the best of their illustrious fathers in this little detail and, like me, will be mediocre people, very much inferior to their fathers. We will explain laboriously how those charming men of wit should proceed in order to be even more sublime. They, meanwhile, will continue to write sublime things, while we are just barely able to write pamphlets.

6.

I have been told: *Poetry is the ideal beauty in expression.* Given a thought, poetry is *the most beautiful way* of rendering it—the way in which it will have *the most* effect.

I deny this as regards tragedy—at least for that tragedy which gets its effects from an exact rendering of the emotions and the events of life.

In the dramatic genre, which in this respect is opposed to the epic poem, the thought or feeling must first of all be expressed with clarity.

When the measure of the verse does not allow of the *precise word* that a deeply aroused person would use in a given situation, what will you do? You will betray the feeling for the alexandrine, as Racine often does. The reason for this is simple. Very few persons know enough about feelings to say: "This is the right word that you are neglecting. The one you are using is only a weak synonym." But the most stupid person in the audience knows very well what makes a line of poetry rough or harmonious. He knows even better (because all his vanity depends upon it) which word is noble diction and which one is not.

The person who speaks noble language is of the court, everybody else is *low-born.* It turns out that two-thirds of the language, since it cannot be used on the stage except by *low-borns,* does not belong to the noble style.[8]

[7] An ignoble tone in 1788; but one which, in my opinion, once again became vigorous and true in 1823, as it perhaps was in 1650, before the court had purified and sifted the language, as Goethe puts it so well (p. 117).

[8] Laharpe, *Cours de littérature.*

Yesterday (March 26), at a concert at the Opéra, as the orchestra was murdering the duet from Rossini's *Armide,* my neighbor said to me: "It's detestable! It's scandalous!" Astounded, I replied: "You are quite right." "It's scandalous," he continued, "that the musicians are not wearing knee breeches!" There you have the French public and decorum as the court has taught it to us.

I believe I can conclude that when the expression of the thought is susceptible of no other beauty than a *perfect clarity,* poetry is out of place.

It is the function of poetry to concentrate in one place, by means of ellipses, inversions, combinations of words, etc. (the privileges of poetry), those things that cause us to be struck by a beauty of nature. But in drama it is the *preceding scenes* that make us *feel* the word we hear spoken in the immediate scene. For example, Talma saying to his friend:

> Do you know the handwriting of Rutilius?
>
> Manlius

If the character, by means of poetic expression, tries to add to the force of what he says, he drops to the level of a mere speechmaker *whom I mistrust.* This is the great defect of those dramatic poets who make a show of their style.

If the character gives the slightest indication that he is thinking of his style, distrust makes its appearance, sympathy flies out of the window, and dramatic pleasure disappears.

With regard to dramatic pleasure, if I had to choose between two extremes, I should always prefer prose that was too simple (like that of Sedaine or Goldoni) to poetry which was too beautiful.

We must always remember that the dramatic action takes place in a room, one wall of which has been removed by the magic wand of Melpomene and replaced by the orchestra and box-seats, thanks to the magic wand of a fairy. The characters do not know that there is an audience. From the moment they make *apparent* concessions to that audience, they are no longer characters: they are rhapsodists reciting an epic poem that may be more or less beautiful.

Inversion is a great *concession* in French, an immense privilege of poetry, in this language friendly to truth and clear before it is anything else.

The dominance of rhythm, or of the poetic line, begins only when inversion is allowed.

Poetry is admirably suited to the epic poem, to satire, to satirical comedy, and to a certain kind of tragedy written for the courtiers.

A man of the court will always go into ecstasies at the nobility of this communication from Agamemnon to his gentleman of the chamber, Arcas:

> Tu vois mon trouble, apprends ce qui le cause,
> Et juge s'il est temps, ami, que je repose.
> Tu te souviens du jour qu'en Aulide assemblés, etc.

> (You see my anxiety; now hear its cause and judge, my friend, whether it is time for me to rest. You remember the day when, at Aulis assembled . . .)

Iphigénie, Act I, Scene i

If, instead of using the word *Tragedies,* you are willing to entitle Racine's works *Dialogues Excerpted from an Epic Poem,* I will exclaim along with you: "It is sublime!" Those dialogues served as tragedy for the *courtly* nation of 1670; but they are no longer tragedies for the reasoning, industrial population of 1823.

The usual rejoinder to this is a personal insult more or less disguised in very polite terms: "Your soul is not of a kind to appreciate the beauty of poetry." Nothing is more possible. And if such is the case, my arguments will soon be disregarded, like those of a blind man who attempts to argue about colors.

All I want to say is that to me, a modern Frenchman who has never seen costumes of satin and whom despotism has compelled to wander over Europe from childhood and to endure no slight hardships, the characters of Racine, Alfieri, Manzoni, and Schiller always have the look of people who are *pleased that they can speak so well.* That they are fired with passion, I will readily agree. But first and foremost they are pleased with their own eloquence.

In the first part of *Racine and Shakespeare* I said that we now need tragedies in prose. To this came the reply that I was a fool.[9] I was told: "Your soul is not of a kind to appreciate the beauty of poetry." No matter. Let us wait for two years and see whether others will take up the ideas expressed in this pamphlet. I am like that soldier from Mainz who, in 1814, assumed the title of "General Garrison" and commanded the troops for three days. I have no reputation. I am nothing if I am alone. I am nothing if no one follows me. But I am everything if the public says to itself: "That man has brought forth an idea." I am either nothing, or else I am the voice of a public that has been afraid to speak out for fear of the great ghost of Racine. Do you really think I do not realize the absurdity of a clock that, at midday, has its hands pointing to 4:00 P.M.? I am speaking out because I see clearly that the hour of *classicism* has struck. The courtiers have disappeared; the pedants are dying out or becoming police censors; and *classicism* is vanishing.

7.

I remember meeting one day, in Koenigsberg, a French author of my acquaintance: a man of intelligence, full of vanity, an author type if there ever was one, but still a rather good writer—excepting only the fact that he does not know a word of French. He read me a pamphlet that was very amusing in its own way. When I exhorted him to use the words and turns of phrase one finds in Rousseau, La Bruyère, *et al.*, he turned red with anger and said: "It is plain to see that you are an aristocrat. You are a *liberal* in name only. Really! You recognize the authority of forty sterile pedants[10] assembled at the Louvre who think only of nobly granting themselves a pension of six thousand francs or a cross of the Legion of Honor! No, and again no! You are not a liberal. I very much suspected it last night, when I saw how bored

[9] *Pandore,* March 26, 1823.
[10] A reference to the Académie Française. [Translator's note.]

you were in the company of those four honest grain merchants from Hamburg. Do you know what you really need? You need salons and *marquis* to applaud you. Come on, now. You're a doomed man. You will never love our country, and you will be like a lukewarm type all your life."

This anger on the part of a childhood friend pleased me a great deal. In it, I saw the absurdity of the human species nakedly exposed. I gave him a few bad and inconclusive answers in order to enjoy the situation to the fullest and let him expatiate at length. If I had wanted to talk sense, I would have said: "I would share your contempt for the forty gentlemen concerned (this was in 1806) if they spoke in their own names. But they are astute fellows who have long been skillful at listening. They bend a very sharp ear to the voice of the public. Actually, the forty of them are merely the secretaries of the public in matters relating to the language. They are never concerned with ideas, merely with the manner of expressing them. Their job is to note the successive changes in words and turns of phrase as they observe them in the salons. Because they are worshippers of everything that is antiquated, a new usage must be very well confirmed and quite incontestable before they will consent to undergo the pain of admitting it into their dictionary. This is the virtue of a secretary, and I respect them for it."

One should not make innovations in language, because language is a thing agreed upon. That thing over there is called a *table*. If I began to refer to it as an *asphocèle*, that would be a brilliant invention indeed. The little bird hopping about under the eaves is called a *titmouse*. Would it be especially pleasant to call it a *noras?*

The same thing holds for the *turns of phrase* in a language, as for its words. In La Bruyère and Pascal I find a certain turn of phrase to express *astonishment and contempt* mixed together in equal portions. What is the purpose in inventing a new turn of phrase? We should leave this glory to Madame de Staël, and to MM. de Chateaubriand, de Marchangy, le vicomte d'Arlincourt, *et al.* Certainly it is more pleasant, and requires less time, to invent a phrase than to search laboriously for it in a *Lettre provinciale* or a harangue of Patru.

I am afraid that the most remote posterity, when it comes to deal with these great writers, will relegate them to the rank of the Senecas and the Lucans, whom we understand less easily than Cicero and Vergil. It is true that posterity will be recompensed for its trouble by the sublimity of their thoughts. Perhaps, however, posterity will regret that these great writers, who thought better than did Voltaire and Rousseau, did not use the same language. In that case they would have combined all of the best features together.

A language is constituted just as much by its *turns of phrase* as by its words. Whenever there already exists a turn of phrase that clearly expresses a certain idea, why produce a new one? One gives the reader a little tickling of surprise. This is the way to palm off ideas that are commonplace or worn out. Even today, people will still read two pages of M. l'abbé Delille for the pleasure of guessing riddles or seeing how one says "wine press" in the noble style. Likewise, I notice that the druggist on the corner, with a view to ennobling himself, has had the following painted on his house in gilt letters: *Pharmacie de M. Fleurant.*

The conceited ass from the provinces, when telling the story of his conquests, is hard put to know whether he should say: "I came across Madame So-and-So, whom I had seduced in the country, *dans la société*" or *"dans le monde"* or *"dans les salons."*

In speaking of his fiancée, he doesn't know whether he should say: *"C'est une fort jolie fille"* or *"C'est une jolie demoiselle"* or *"C'est une jeune personne fort jolie."* His embarrassment is great, because there are good vaudeville couplets that make a joke of all these locutions.

We may have to be *romantic* in our ideas, because the age will have it so; but let us be *classical* in our expressions and turns of phrase. These are matters of convention; that is, virtually unchangeable, or at any rate only changeable at a very slow rate.

We should allow ourselves—and only occasionally, at the

very most—nothing more than the kind of ellipsis Voltaire and Rousseau longed to use, which seems to give one's style more rapidity. And even then, I am not altogether certain that this little bit of license may not render us unintelligible to posterity.

8.

Concerning Taste

What is taste?
Goethe replies:

It is that which is fashionable. In writing, it is the art of pleasing to the utmost, today. It is the art of knotting one's tie well in productions of the intellect.

The characteristic trait of the genius is the ability to produce new ideas in abundance.[11] His pride is such that he prefers creating a new thought—giving the public a new insight for which one would search in vain in any earlier volume—to dressing up and giving a pleasing appearance to some new idea he has just come across. But the man of genius does not produce without a purpose. As a scholar, he intends that his works should enlighten other men; as a writer, that they should give them enjoyment. Here is the starting point for the action and work of *taste,* an intermediary placed between the ideal world, where the genius walks alone, accompanied only by his conceptions, and the real, outer world where he intends to produce them. *Taste* examines the ethical state of the country and of the age, the common prejudices, the opinions in vogue, and the ruling passions. In accordance with the results of this examination, it teaches the genius what conventions and proprieties to observe, and shows him how he should order his compositions and in what forms he should present his ideas in order to make the most vivid and enjoyable impression on the public. When one and the same man possesses this double advantage—genius, the powerful creator, and taste, the skillful arranger—he becomes one

---

[11] *Hommes Célèbres de France au dix-huitième siècle,* page 100.

of those fortunate writers, the admiration of youth. In this case his success overtakes and surpasses his hopes, and his talent reigns as a sovereign over the minds and hearts of everyone. But if he combines them (these two faculties) only to an unequal degree, both his successes and his works will suffer from this lack of fidelity to what is fashionable.

The entire mediocre and quasi-mediocre portion of the public fails to see these new ideas. He [the genius] produces his effect on certain minds, and fails to produce it on others. This inequality between genius and taste in one and the same talent, gives rise on the part of the public to the most contradictory judgments. Those who perceive only his shortcomings are indignant that others should find things of beauty in his work. They depreciate him below his real value and would like to destroy him. And their disparagement is sincere. Those whom similar circumstances, in their earlier life, have made sympathetic to the spirit of our author are more moved by what is good in his work than offended by its imperfections. They generously attribute to him everything that he lacks, try in some way to supplement it, and by means of their praises elevate him to a level which he has not actually attained. All of them are wrong. The genius remains what he is, regardless of our accidental dispositions toward him. Neither vengeance for the boredom he has caused us nor gratitude for the pleasure he has given us can enrich him by attributing to him that which he does not possess; he is impoverished when one takes away from him that which he possesses.

In the sixteenth century, the French had a poet named Du Bartas, who at that time was very much admired by them. His fame spread throughout Europe, and he was translated into several languages. His poem on the seven days of the Creation, written in seven *chants* and entitled *La Semaine,* went through thirty editions in five years. Du Bartas was a *man of taste* for the year 1590. Today, reading his naïve and rather too long descriptions, the most insignificant journalist would exclaim: *"What execrable taste!"* And he would be right, just as people were right in 1590—so local and momentary is taste, and so true is it that what is admired on one side of the Rhine is often despised on the other, and that the masterpieces of one century are the laughingstock of the next.

The events of the literary revolution that cast Du Bartas into oblivion and disregard are easy to see. When the *grands seigneurs* who had lived at their widely scattered châteaux, where they were often a cause of fear to the kings,[12] had been called to the court by Richelieu, who tried to disarm them and who kept them in that one place by flattering and irritating their vanity, it soon became an honor to live at court.[13] Almost immediately, the language showed a marked trend toward purification. *The progress of taste* consisted in perfecting the forms of style, which became more and more classical and were based on the study and imitation of the models of antiquity. There was a scrupulous and almost minute *purification* that *sifted* the language, if one may so express it, and that resulted in the rejection—as *lacking in dignity,* and being a sure sign of *inferior* rank in the person who used them—of a large number of words, phrases, and *even ideas* which had been contained in books before this purification. It is probably true that the French language has been compensated for the losses it suffered as a result of such rigorous purism, by the acquisition of a few new stylistic forms that are irreproachable in the eyes of criticism. Still, I believe that the language lost a great many picturesque and imitative expressions,[14] and that it was more purged than enriched by this operation of *taste.*

In this entire revolution, described by Goethe in 1805, and in the habits that it necessarily implanted, do we not see the source of the *pedantic trait* so evident today in our literary men of a certain age? The pedants of the age of Louis XV no longer accepted new things except from young courtiers and

---

[12] The *Mémoires* of Bassompierre.
[13] The autobiography of Agrippa d'Aubigné.
[14] Which M. P.-L. Courier, author of the *Petition* for the peasants who have been forbidden to dance, is trying to bring back into the language today, in his translation of Herodotus.

from what they called *le bel usage*. If those young courtiers had been pedants like the young English peers who are graduated from Oxford or Cambridge, it would have meant the end of the French language. It would have become a kind of *Sanskrit,* a language of priests, a privileged idiom. It would never have spread throughout Europe.

Among a nation of people who are more rational than sensitive, who have decided opinions and tenacious prejudices, and who bring to the pleasures of the intellect more *pedantry* than enthusiasm, the genius is obliged to conform to the narrow rules prescribed for him, and to walk in the path marked out for him. He is subjected to laws rather than making them. The features of his face scarcely show through the mask he is required to wear. When this happens, taste is a tyrant, and genius is a slave. This is the situation in which the majority of French authors have found themselves.[15]

9.

Certain persons who know of no other way to refute an argument than to attribute absurdities to their opponents, have had the kindness to quote me as saying that *Racine's works should be burned.*

A great man, in whatever form he has left an imprint of his soul to posterity, always makes that form immortal. In one way or another—whether in drawing, like Hogarth,[16] or in music, like Cimarosa—such a man has given us the impressions made by nature on his heart. Those *impressions* are priceless, both for those who, lacking the intelligence to see nature *in nature,* nonetheless find a good deal of it when looking at copies in the works of famous artists, and for those who see nature, who adore its aspects, as they vary from the poignant to the sublime, and who learn more fully

[15] Goethe, *Les Hommes Célèbres de France,* p. 109.
[16] Famous English painter and engraver; born in 1697, died in 1764. He excelled in the accurate depiction of the passions and popular scenes.

to appreciate certain of its details by surrendering their souls to the *effect* of the works of the great masters who have depicted those details. This is to say that my political opinion, which I find in my journal, is fortified by that much.

After I hear the duet, *Io ti lascio perchè uniti,* from the first part of Cimarosa's *Il Matrimonio segreto,* my heart becomes aware of new nuances in the spectacle of love thwarted by ambition. In particular, the duet puts me into a state wherein I can set aside certain vulgar circumstances that often obstruct emotion. When I see a pair of unhappy lovers, I tell myself: "It is like the scene in *Il Matrimonio segreto* when Carolina says to her lover, *'Io ti lascio.'*" Immediately, everything of a vulgar nature in the story of the poor lovers I see in the salon disappears, and I am touched. I owe this delicious moment—and perhaps the good deed it may inspire in me—to the existence of Cimarosa.

I trust that I have now dotted all my *i*'s well, and that no more absurdities will be attributed to me. At the very most, the people of no feeling will deride my tears. But it has been a long time, now, since I took my stand; and we have long seemed ridiculous to one another. Should I try to change myself because my neighbor is different from me?

In a thousand years, among nations yet to be born, Racine will still be admirable:

1) For having often depicted human nature in an astonishing way. Not in Agamemnon's pseudo-pun, *"Vous y serez,*[17] *ma fille,"* but in Hermione's sublime rejoinder to Orestes (who has notified her of the death of Pyrrhus), *"Who told you?"* Also, in the heavenly role of Monime, which has very rightly been called "antique sculpture"; and in the regrets of Phaedra:

> Hélas! du crime affreux dont la honte me suit
> Jamais mon triste coeur n'a recueilli le fruit.
> Jusqu'au dernier soupir de malheurs poursuivie,
> Je rends dans les tourments une pénible vie.

(Alas! My sorrowing heart never plucked the fruit of the frightful crime whose shame pursues me! A prey to

[17] Meaning both "you will be there" and "you will get it." [Translator's note.]

102

misfortunes until my last breath, I shall render up, in torment, my grief-laden life.)

Act IV, Scene vi

2) In this same sublime tragedy of *Phèdre,* the nurse of that princess, who has been the constant companion of the latter since her birth and loves her as her own child, when she has to report the frightful detail that her little girl has not taken any food for three days, speaks the following admirable lines:

OENONE

. . .

Rebelle à tous nos soins, sourde à tous nos discours,
Voulez-vous sans pitié laisser finir vos jours?
Quelle fureur les borne au milieu de leur course?
Quel charme ou quel poison en a tari la source?
Les ombres par trois fois ont obscuri les cieux
Depuis que le sommeil n'est entré dans vos yeux;
Et le jour a trois fois chassé la nuit obscure
Depuis que votre corps languit sans nourriture, etc., etc.

(Disdainful of our concern, and deaf to whatever we say, do you want to let your life come to an end without having shown any pity? What folly is cutting it off in the middle of its course? What witchcraft or poison has dried up its source? Thrice have the shades of night darkened the skies since last sleep entered your eyes. And thrice has the day driven off the dark night while your body has languished without food, etc., etc.)

Act I, Scene iii

Admire, if you can, the idea of "dark" added to that of "night" at such a moment! Well! There is no doubt that the persons of *refined taste* at the court of Versailles thought that was very beautiful. They were obliged to avoid the bourgeois expression "for three days," which would have totally prevented them from being emotionally moved. And whatever one is, a king or a shepherd, on the throne or carrying a staff, one is always right in feeling things the way one feels them and in finding beautiful that which gives pleasure.

Subsequently, French taste was formed *after the model* of Racine. For a century, rhetoricians went into ecstasies *in a witty manner* over the idea that Racine had perfect *taste*. They closed their eyes to all objections; for example, to the deed of Andromache when she has another child killed in order to save her son, Astyanax. Orestes informs us of this:

> J'apprends que, pour ravir son enfance au supplice,
> Andromaque trompa l'ingénieux Ulysse,
> Tandis qu'un autre enfant, arraché de ses bras,
> Sous le nom de son fils fut conduit au trépas.

> (I have learned that Andromache, in order to save her child from torture, deceived the wily Ulysses, while another child, torn from her arms, was mistaken for her son and led to his death.)

Andromaque, Act I, Scene i

The other child, however, also had a mother, who probably cried—unless they were thoughtful enough to take him to the hospital. But what do her tears matter? They were ridiculous, because she was a woman of the *third estate*. It was only too great an honor for her, was it not, to sacrifice her son in order to save *his young master*?[18]

All this must seem very beautiful to a Russian prince with one hundred thousand francs of income and thirty thousand serfs.

Thus the most remote posterity will also admire Racine for having created the best possible tragedy for the vain and witty courtiers of a despot who was himself very vain and very egotistical, but a reasonable man, very much concerned with playing a fine role in Europe and skillful at utilizing great men and putting them in the right positions. Wherever monarchy reproduces itself, Racine will have his admirers. Literarily speaking, when Iturbide tried to establish an imperial

[18] A remark of the Marquis de Bonald for the Duc de Bordeaux, in December, 1822. Cf. M. Alessandro Manzoni, in the translation by M. Fauriel.

throne in Mexico, he was merely inaugurating a course in literature in favor of Racine. If he had succeeded, our booksellers would have been able to ship crates of Laharpe off to Mexico quite safely. Likewise, after the lapse of so many centuries, we understand what Herodotus is saying, and we admire the behavior of Pharnasses [Prexaspes?], a courtier of Cambyses, when the latter kills Prexaspes' son without the slightest qualm.[19]

In its most ambitious claims, romanticism asks only that prose tragedy be allowed to compete in the ordinary manner.

This involves no Jesuitic policy and no ulterior motive. Here is mine [my policy] in its entirety. Mythological tragedy will always be written in verse. The pomp and majesty of beautiful poetic lines will probably always be required in order to throw a convenient veil over the absurdity of the fatalism[20] of *Oedipus* or *Phèdre*, leaving us aware only of the beautiful effects derived from these premises. For example, the mutual secret-sharing of Oedipus and Jocasta (Act IV, Scene i). Also, tragedies of love, such as *Andromaque, Tancrède, Ariane,* and *Inès de Castro* will perhaps always go better in verse.[21]

We insist upon prose only for tragedies on national themes: the death of Henri III, the return from Elba, Clovis gaining a foothold in Gaul with the help of the priests,[22] Charles IX, or the salutary rigor (massacre) of Saint Bartholomew's Day. Any of these subjects, when treated in alexandrine lines, is as though masked. This is mathematically demonstrable, because two-thirds of the language spoken today in the most refined salons cannot be used on the stage.

[19] Herodotus, Book III, in the colorful translation by P.-L. Courier.
[20] A fatalism entirely reproduced by *Multi sunt vocati, pauci vero electi.* Jupiter was not malicious like Jehovah, because he had Fate above him.
[21] The three last-named plays are by Voltaire, Corneille, and La Motte, respectively. [Translator's note.]
[22] I have just read about that astounding revolution in the naïve chronicle of St. Gregory of Tours. Our hypocrites have blamed M. Dulaure for having been just as naïve in his *Histoire de Paris.* What astounds me is that they have not resorted to the irresistible argument of Sainte Pélagie (Prison)—actually the only good argument in such a cause.

I defy anyone to reply to that objection. But whatever the immense prestige of the pedants—though they may have dominion over public education, the Academy, and even the booksellers—they have a terrible enemy in the dialogue-type debates at the Chamber of Deputies and the dramatic interest they often arouse. The nation is hungry for its historical tragedy. On the day of the expulsion of M. Manuel,[23] it is impossible for the nation to be satisfied with a performance of *Zaïre* at the Théâtre-Français and not to consider as downright silly that sultan who is going *to give an hour to the business of his empire*. The grim Richard III would be much more to the point. *L'amour-passion* can exist only among idle persons; and as for *galanterie*, I am afraid Louis XVI killed it forever in France when he summoned the assembly of the *notables*.

Racine was a romantic: he wrote tragedies that gave real pleasure to the Dangeaus, the Cavoyes, the La Fayettes, and the Cayluses. The absurd thing is that people writing in 1823 should try to grasp and to reproduce the character traits and forms that were found pleasing about 1670. Such people are doubly ridiculous: with respect to their own age, which they do not understand, and with respect to the seventeenth century, whose taste they will never grasp.

For some years now, all the arts in France, poetry included, have been mere trades. Every young man of eighteen who has won his prizes at school, who was not born absolutely devoid of intelligence, and who—unhappily for his friends—sets about becoming a poet, learns by heart four thousand lines of Racine and fifteen hundred lines of Delille. He struggles at it for a few years, courts the favor of the newspapers, grows thin and spiteful, and finally, after five or six years, he is a poet. That is, he composes poems that are fairly good in appearance. There is nothing in them that one can find fault with. But after twenty lines our ideas lose their vividness; after a hundred lines we are struggling to keep our eyes open; and somewhere toward line two hundred we cease to listen. Still, the unfortunate fellow is no less a poet for all

[23] On March 3, 1823, on a motion by M. de la Bourdonnaye, the Chamber of Deputies voted the expulsion of M. Manuel.

this. If he practices intrigue, he will be successful; and once that happens, he will devote the rest of his life to envy and unhappiness. I have been assured that there are three thousand five hundred poets among the young people living in Paris.

RACINE AND SHAKESPEARE II

or A Reply to the Manifesto against Romanticism
Delivered by
M. Auger at a Formal Session of the Institute

THE OLD MAN: "Let us continue."
THE YOUNG MAN: "Let us examine."
There you have the entire nineteenth century.

Foreword

NEITHER M. AUGER nor myself is well known to the public. So much the worse for this pamphlet. Also, it was a good nine or ten months ago that M. Auger made the bombastic and rather meaningless attack on romanticism to which I am replying. M. Auger was speaking in the name of the Académie Française. When, on the second of last May, I had completed my reply, I experienced a kind of bashfulness at the idea of maltreating a body that used to be so highly regarded and to which Racine and Fénelon had belonged.

We have, in France, a most unusual sentiment at the bottom of our hearts—one I did not even suspect that I had, so blinded was I by the political theories of America. A man who is after a certain position publishes a piece of libel in the newspapers. You refute it with a modest exposition of the facts. He swears once again that his libel is the truth and boldly signs his letter. (After all, in terms of fastidiousness and flower of reputation, what does he have to lose?) He calls upon you to sign your answer, and that is where the trouble really begins. You may cite the most incontrovertible arguments, but to no avail: he will make reply. And so you will have to go on writing and signing, and little by little you will find yourself in the mud. The public will insist upon seeing you side by side with your adversary.

Well! In daring to jape the Academy about the bad faith of the speech that it put into the mouth of its director, I feared I might be taken for a most impudent man. I have no desire to be one of those persons who attack the ridiculous things that gently bred people have agreed to let pass without comment in society.

Last May, this objection to the publication of my romantic pamphlet seemed to me unanswerable. Happily, the Academy has since been careless enough to make such a singular choice of a new member—and a choice that betrays so plainly the influence of gastronomy—that everybody has been making fun of it. Thus I shall not be the first. Actually, in a country where there is an *opposition*, there can be no more Académie Française, because the ministry will never permit the great talents of the opposition to be admitted into the Academy, and the public will stubbornly continue to be unjust toward the noble writers paid by the ministers whose Academy will be Les Invalides.

Preface

ONE DAY five or six months ago the Académie Française was moving along at the slow and almost imperceptible gait that takes it gently and safely toward the end of the monotonous work of the continuation of its dictionary. Everyone was asleep except the permanent secretary and the rapporteur, Auger, when by some chance the word "romantic" came up.

At the mention of this fatal name of an insolent and disorderly faction, the general torpor gave way to a much more lively feeling. It must have been something like what would have happened if an accident favorable to the maintenance of sound doctrine had suddenly brought Luther or Calvin up in front of the great inquisitor, Torquemada, surrounded by judges and favorites of the Inquisition. Immediately, one would have seen a single thought on all those faces, otherwise so different. Everyone would have asked: "By what sufficiently cruel tortures can we kill him?"

I feel all the more free to allow myself such a grim image, because one certainly cannot imagine anything more innocent than forty personages, grave and respected, who suddenly appoint themselves the *very impartial* judges of a new cult opposed to that of which they have made themselves the priests. Most assuredly, it is in good conscience that they condemn the profaners who are causing trouble for this happy cult, which, in exchange for little thoughts arranged in pretty phrases, provides them with all the advantages that the government of a great nation can confer: ribbons, pensions, honors, positions as censors, etc., etc. The behavior of people ordinarily so prudent might, of course, recall a famous witticism of the greatest of those men of genius whom they so ludicrously attempt to honor by their periodic homilies—but a genius so free in his departures from the true path, and so little prone to respect ridiculous things, that for a century the Academy refused to admit, not his person, but his portrait. Molière, whom everyone has named by this time, puts the following well-known line into the mouth of a goldsmith who thinks there is nothing quite so pretty, to cheer up and cure a sick person, as large wrought-gold objects displayed in the sickroom: "But you're in the trade, Mr. Josse." [1]

However classic and lacking in *novelty* this joke may be, it most certainly would have met with severe disapproval if anyone had mentioned it that day when the Academy was suddenly jerked out of its customary torpor by the voice of the rapporteur for its dictionary, calling out the fatal word "romantic" between the words "rosemary" [*romarin*] and "Romanist." M. Auger reads his definition. But he is immediately interrupted by voices from all parts of the room. Everybody is eager to suggest a few vigorous phrases to beat down the monster. But they actually belong rather to the style of Juvenal than to that of Horace or Boileau. It is a question of clearly designating these wild innovators who are foolishly claiming that the time might come—and perhaps even in our day, alas!—when people could write works more interesting and less boring than those of Messieurs de l'Académie. The very noble pleasure of insulting defenseless enemies soon puts the academicians into a state of poetic rapture. Prose no longer suffices for the general enthusiasm. The amiable author of *Les Etourdis* and so many other dull comedies is requested to read a satire he has recently written against the romantics. To describe the success enjoyed by such a poem in such a place would be superfluous.

When the Conscript Fathers of Literature had finally recovered somewhat from the inextinguishable laughter awakened in those noble souls by abuse heaped upon absent rivals, they resumed with gravity the course of their official operations. They began by unanimously declaring themselves competent to judge the romantics. Then three of their most violent members were assigned to prepare the definition of the word "romanticism." One hopes that particular care will be given to the preparation of this article because, by a happenstance that is not at all surprising, this item of twelve

[1] Literally, *Vous êtes orfèvre, Monsieur Josse.* From *L'Amour médecin,* Act I, Scene i. [Translator's note.]

lines will be the first literary work of these three men of letters.

This most memorable session, during which somebody actually said something interesting, was about to come to an end when one of the Forty rose to his feet and said: "All the absurdity of those literary pygmies, the barbarous abettors of the savage Shakespeare—a ridiculous poet whose vagabond muse transports the ideas, the manners,[2] and the speech of the London bourgeois to all times and places—has just been exposed, gentlemen, with an eloquence at least equal to your impartiality. Before, you were only the preservers of taste; now you are going to be its avengers. But when will that sweet moment of vengeance arrive? Perhaps in four or five years, when we publish this dictionary that Europe is awaiting with a respectful impatience. Now I ask you, gentlemen. In a nation that has recently fallen a prey to the fatal madness of submitting everything to discussion—not only the laws of the State but, what is much worse, the glory of her academies—is there any limit to the immense progress that error and false taste can make in four years? I ask that on the twenty-fourth of next April—on the solemn occasion of the joint meeting of the four academies—that you appoint one of yourselves to proclaim, to a nation eager to hear you, our decree on romanticism. Have no fear, gentlemen. That decree will kill the monster."

Unanimous applause marked the end of this speech. M. Auger, an academician whose adoration of the rules is all the more rigid in that he has never written anything, was unanimously chosen to crush romanticism.

A week passed. M. Auger appeared on the rostrum. There was a crowd in the hall: thirteen members were present. Several had put on their costumes. Before unrolling his manuscript, the director of the Academy addressed the following words to that honorable assembly:

All extreme measures, gentlemen, border upon extreme dangers. In paying to the romantics the signal honor of

[2] Page 14 of the *Manifesto*.

115

mentioning them within these walls, you will make known the existence of that insolent sect in certain venerable salons into which, previously, the name of the monster had not penetrated. This peril, great as it may seem to you, is in my view merely the precursor of an extreme danger at the sight of which—and I am not afraid to say it, gentlemen—you will perhaps decide to deprive the French people of the great lesson that you were preparing on the solemn occasion of April 24. The celebrated Dr. Johnson among the English, more than a half-century ago; the poet Metastasio among the Italians, at about the same time; in our day, M. le marquis Visconti; M. Schlegel, that German of such disastrous fame who once gave Madame de Staël the cruel idea of making herself the apostle of a doctrine baneful to the national glory, and even more baneful for the Academy; and twenty others I could mention were I not afraid of tiring you with too many enemy names, have published truths—only too clear today, alas!—on romanticism in general and on the nature of theatrical illusion in particular. These truths are only too well suited to dazzle the people of society, because they throw a dangerous light on the impressions that those people go to seek at the theatre every day. These disastrous truths tend toward nothing less, gentlemen, than heaping ridicule upon our celebrated UNITY OF PLACE—the keystone of the entire classical system. In refuting them, I would run the risk of making them known. Therefore, I have followed what seemed to me the wisest course, and treated them as *never having happened*. I have not made the slightest mention of them in my speech. . . . (Interruption; unanimous applause.)

On every hand there are exclamations of "A great measure! A profound policy!" And a Jesuit murmurs, "We couldn't have done it any better ourselves."

The speaker continued:

Gentlemen, we must not grant the freedom of the city to those baneful doctrines that have brought fame to the

Johnsons,[3] the Viscontis, the contributors to the *Edinburgh Review,* and a hundred others. Let us reproach them—en masse only, and without naming them—with a ridiculous obscurity. Instead of saying "the Prussians" and "the Saxons," like everyone else, let us say "the Bructeri" and "the Sicambri." [4] All defenders of sound doctrine will applaud such erudition. In passing, we should deride the ridiculous poverty of those good German writers who are *inclined toward error by their sincerity.*[5] In an age when a *book review* pays very handsomely and a *report* brings unlimited success, they are content (with what I would term a very niggardly taste) to lead a frugal and quiet life, which forever cuts them off from the pomp of the courts and the brilliant positions one can obtain there with only a modicum of savoir-faire and compliancy. Those poor men offer the gothic and very unacademic excuse that they want to keep the privilege of speaking the truth, as they see it, on any subject. And they add—those poor Sicambri who have never occupied positions of any importance under any regime: not even *censors* or bureau chiefs—that dangerous maxim that subverts all proprieties in literature: RIDENDO DICERE VERUM QUID VETAT? (If a thing seems to us to be true, why not say it with a laugh?)

Gentlemen, at the mention of this phrase on the ridiculous, I can see a dark cloud spreading over your faces, which usually wear such glad expressions. I can surmise what you are thinking about. You are remembering certain pamphlets published by a *wine grower,*[6] which tend toward nothing less than direspect toward all that is most respect-

[3] See the famous *Preface* to the *Complete Works of Shakespeare,* published in 1765; the examination of the question: *In what does theatrical illusion consist?*
[4] Page 20 of the *Manifesto.*
[5] Page 5 of M. Auger's speech.
[6] The reference is to Paul-Louis Courier, soldier by profession, Hellenist and pamphleteer by avocation, whom Stendhal very much admired. Upon being refused admission to the Institute (to succeed his recently deceased father-in-law), he composed his famous tract, *Lettre à Messieurs de l'Académie des Inscriptions et Belles-Lettres.* [Translator's note.]

able in this world—all that is most esteemed among men. I refer to the choices of the Académie des Inscriptions and the very memorable admission into this learned body of MM. Jomard and le Prévot-d'Iray. There is not the slightest doubt about it, gentlemen: the monster of romanticism respects no proprieties whatsoever. From the fact that a thing has never been done, it concludes (and I tremble at the thought), not that one should carefully abstain from it, but, on the contrary, that it might be interesting to try it. And however respectable the costume that a man of letters has managed to clothe himself in, it will make bold to mock him. These miserable romantics have made their appearance in literature for the sole purpose of upsetting our lives. Once our colleague, le Prévot-d'Iray, had been admitted, who could have told him that anyone would demand of him that prize-winning *Mémoire* that he had promised never to publish?

If a romantic were present here today, there is no doubt, gentlemen, but that he would take the liberty of writing a ridiculous account of our work, so important to the national glory, in some miserable pamphlet. I know very well that we will say that there is a scandalous lack of taste in such writings—that they are *crude*. Following an official example, we may even go so far as to call them *cynical*. But you see, gentlemen, how everything changes. Forty years ago a remark like this would have been enough to spell the ruin, not only of the most carefully documented book, but of its author as well. Alas! A short time ago this word *cynical*, applied to the writings of a certain *wine grower*—a man of no consequence who does not even own a carriage—served only to make his pamphlet sell twenty thousand copies. You see, gentlemen, the insolence of the public and all the perils of our position. Let us be wise enough to refuse the delectable pleasure of vengeance. Let us be wise enough to reply only by the silence of scorn to all these romantic authors writing to meet the demands of a revolutionary century and capable (I haven't the slightest doubt) of considering forty solemn personages who assemble on certain scheduled days, in order to do nothing and to tell one another that they are the most remarkable people in the nation, as nothing more than *big children playing at being grownups.*

At this point, M. Auger was interrupted by shouts of "Bravo!" But in resolving to continue writing as little as possible, the illustrious academicians seem to have decided to redouble their verbosity. There was such a crowd of orators that it took four consecutive sessions to approve the manifesto drawn up by M. Auger. There is the case of one modifier used either before or after the noun, *which it weakens,* which changed position seven times and was the subject of five amendments.[7]

I must admit that this manifesto puts me in a difficult position. In order to guarantee it against any refutation, the gentlemen of the Academy employed a degree of skill that was extraordinary and well worthy of men admired throughout Paris for political success applied to the interests of private life. If these gentlemen had merely been writers of brilliant intellect—just ordinary successors of Voltaire, La Bruyère, and Boileau—they would have tried to marshal invincible arguments in their document, and to make them intelligible to everyone by a clear and simple style. What would have happened in this case? These arguments would have been attacked by opposing arguments, and a controversy would have begun. The infallibility of the Academy would have been subjected to doubt, and the prestige it enjoys would have been somewhat damaged in the eyes of people concerned only with yearly income and money in general, who constitute the immense majority in the salons.

In my capacity as a *romantic,* and in order that I might not imitate anybody—not even the Academy—I had the intention of improving such a frivolous discussion by the addition of a very rare and curious thing: a bit of good faith and candor. I simply wanted to begin my refutation by quoting the entirety of M. Auger's manifesto. But alas! My good faith very nearly proved disastrous for me! Good faith, today, is a

[7] This actually happened.

poison one must handle with the greatest care. As soon as I had completed my pamphlet, I read it—or rather, I tried to read it—to a few good friends who were eager to boo my performance. They took their seats, and I opened my notebook and began reading the academic manifesto. But alas! Even before I had got to the sixth page, a deathly chill had spread through my little salon. With my eyes glued to my manuscript, suspecting nothing, I kept on, trying only to go faster. But one of my friends stopped me. He is a young lawyer of robust temperament, battle-hardened from reading documents in legal cases. He was sorely tried in this instance, but he still had the strength to speak. The rest of them had covered their faces with their hands, so that they might give themselves over more completely to their profound concentration. Filled with consternation at this sight, I looked at the young lawyer.

"The elegant phrases you are uttering," he said to me, "are all very well for a solemn assembly. But why is it you don't realize that in a small group of friends there must at least be a show of reason and good faith? When only seven or eight people are present, you can't excuse everything by the necessity of being impressive. Everybody sees only too clearly that nobody else is being fooled. In Paris, when there is a large assembly, people always have the idea that those on the other side of the hall have been taken for dupes and are full of admiration. A session of the Academy is a ceremony. A person comes there worried about finding a seat. Why are so many people in a rush to see something that is merely boring? As soon as the audience is assembled, they start watching the elegant women who are coming in and who take their seats with a lot of to-do. Their next pleasure is trying to recognize the cabinet ministers, present and past, who have deigned to become members of the Academy; and they examine their ribbons and medals. Finally, the thing that saves the speeches made at the Institute is the fact of a show. But you, my friend, if you don't find some other way of beginning your pamphlet than by quoting M. Auger, you are a lost man."

Two of our friends who had been aroused from their revery by our more animated voices, added: "Ah yes! That is very true!" And the lawyer continued: "You must understand that academic phrases are official and therefore designed to *deceive somebody*. For this reason it is not a good idea to read them to a small group of good friends—especially when they are persons of equal rank."

"Ah!" I replied, *"Le Constitutionnel* gave me good warning, if only I had understood it, that M. Auger was a *wise and cool* critic (the *Constitutionnel* for April 26). Judging from the effect on you, they should have said *very cool*. Because after all, gentlemen, apart from the title of my pamphlet, I have not yet read you so much as one sentence of my own. And I won't read you any. I see now that any refutation is impossible, since merely by stating the arguments of my opponents, I put the reader to sleep. Let's go to Tortoni's. It is my duty to make you wake up again; and I most assuredly will not say another word about literature, because I can offer neither pretty women nor honorary decorations to keep your attention."

I said this with a bit of ill humor, vexed at having worked four days for nothing and at having been the dupe of arguments that had struck me as so fine when I wrote them. Whereupon my lawyer friend said: "It is plain to see that you will never succeed at anything. You could spend ten years in Paris without even getting yourself admitted to the Society for Christian Morality or the Academy of Geography! Who said you should not publish your pamphlet? Last night you showed me a letter you had had from one of your *classicist* friends. In four pages, that friend gave you all the arguments that M. Auger should have given in his forty-page article. Publish that letter and your reply. And write a Preface to give the reader an idea of the Jesuitical trick, so full of sly cunning, that the Academy tries to play upon anybody foolhardy enough to attempt a refutation of its *Manifesto*."

"One of two things must happen," the members of Europe's leading literary assemblage told themselves. "Either the obscure person who tries to refute us will not quote us, in which case we will protest his bad faith; or else he will quote the article by that pathetic Auger, and his pamphlet will be disastrously boring. We will tell everybody—we who are forty against one: 'Look how boring and heavy these romantics are, with their alleged refutations.' "

I therefore present to the public the letter in defense of classicism that I received two days after M. Auger's manifesto had made its appearance in the world, by order. This letter contains all the letters [arguments?] made by M. Auger. Thus, in refuting the letter I shall have refuted the manifesto. And this is what I intend to bring home to the least attentive readers, by quoting several sentences of M. Auger as the discussion proceeds.

Will some people criticize me for the tone I have adopted in this Preface? Nothing, it seems to me, is more natural or more simple. What is involved, between M. Auger (who has never accomplished anything) and myself, the undersigned (who likewise has never accomplished anything) is a debate, frivolous in nature and assuredly of no importance to the physical security of the State, on that difficult question: *What direction should be followed in order to write, today, a tragedy that does not make people yawn with boredom after the fourth performance?*

The only difference I can see between myself and M. Auger —of whom I had not read one line until four days ago, when I undertook to refute him—is the fact that there are forty voices, eloquent and respected in society, ready to praise his work. As for me, I would rather risk the criticism of having a rough style than that of having nothing to say. My fault, if I am at fault in this matter, is not that I was unpolished, but that I was polished more quickly.[8]

I have the greatest respect for the Academy as a *constituted assemblage* (Law of 1821). It has *opened* a literary discussion, and I have thought fit to reply. As to those gentlemen among its members whom I have named, I have never had the honor of seeing them. Moreover, I have never tried to offend them in the slightest way. If I have referred to the *renowned* M. Villemain, it was only because I found that word next to his name in *Le Journal des débats*,[9] of which he is the editor.

[8] ". . . *poli plus vite.*" A pun on *poli,* meaning either "polite" or "polished," and on its contrary *impoli.* [Translator's note.]
[9] For March 12, 1823.

The Classicist to the Romantic

April 26, 1824

MY GREATEST THANKS to you, sir, for your thoughtful gift. I shall have your handsome volumes bound as soon as the law on interest rates and the work of the session permit me to do so.

I most earnestly hope that the administration of the Opéra will some day provide, for the listening pleasure of our *dilettanti,* some of the pleasures you describe so well, but I am most dubious of it. The *urlo francese* is much more powerful than Rossini's drums. There is nothing more tenacious than the habits of a public that goes to the theatre only to be relieved of boredom.

I shall not say whether I found anything *romantic* in your work. First of all, one should know what this means. And it seems to me that in order to throw some light on this question, it is time to do away with vague and abstract definitions of things that should be tangible. We should forget the words and look for examples. What is the ROMANTIC? Is it *Han d'Islande,* by that nice old gentleman, Victor Hugo? Is it *Jean Sbogar,* with all those sonorous phrases, by that vaporous writer, Nodier? Is it the famous *Solitaire,* in which one of the most savage warriors in history, after having been killed in battle, takes the trouble to come back to life so that he can run after a fifteen-year-old girl and express his amorous sentiments? Is it that pathetic *Faliero* so outrageously received at the Théâtre-Français, although it was translated from Lord Byron? Is it the *Christophe Colomb* of M. Lemercier, in which (if I recall correctly) the audience, embarked in the Genoese navigator's caravel in the first act, lands on the shores of America in Act Three? Is is the *Panhypocrisiade* by the same poet—a work whose few hundred very well-wrought and very philosophical lines can never make us excuse its monotonous oddity and prodigious intellectual disorder? Is it *La Mort de Socrate*, by Lamartine, *Le Parricide*, by M. Jules Lefèvre, or *Eloa*, the female angel, born of a tear of Jesus Christ, by M. le comte de Vigny? Is it, finally, the false sensitivity, the pretentious elegance, and the compulsory pathos of that swarm of young poets who exploit the *dreamy vein* and the *mysteries of the soul*—and who, well fed and well provided with income, never cease to sing of human miseries and the delights of death? All of these works caused a great stir when they first appeared; all of them have been cited as models in the *new genre;* and all of them are ridiculous today.

I shall not even mention certain works that are downright pitiable, despite the degree of success that heralded their entry into the world. Everyone is familiar with the collusion of the newspapers, the ruses of authors, editions of fifty copies, false titles, sham frontispieces,[1] altered typefaces, etc., etc. All this petty charlatanism was discovered a long time ago. The battle between the romantics and the classicists must be characterized by frankness and generosity. Both have, from time to time, champions who dishonor the cause they claim to be serving. In the matter of style, for example, it would be no more just to reproach your school for having produced the famous *vicomte inversif*,[2] than it would be on your part to blame classicism for having produced a Chapelain or a Pradon. I would not even have cited the aforementioned works as probably belonging to the romantic genre if the majority of those authors had not adorned themselves in society with the handsome name of *romantic writers*—and that with an air of assurance which must cause you no end of despair.

Let us examine the few works which, in the past twenty years, have enjoyed a success confirmed by each passing day. Let us examine *Hector, Tibère, Clytemnestre, Sylla, L'Ecole*

---

[1] Cf. an issue of *Pandore* relative to a debate involving damages between the very lyrical author of *Han* and his publisher, Persan.
[2] Charles Victor Prévot, vicomte d'Arlincourt, a novelist and poet notorious for his abuse of the poetic device of inversion. [Translator's note.]

des Vieilliards, Les Deux gendres, and a few plays by Picard and Duval. Let us examine the different genres, from the novels of Madame Cottin to the songs of Béranger, and we shall have to acknowledge that everything in these works that is good, beautiful, and admired, as regards both style and structure, is in conformity with the precepts and examples of the good writers of the old days, who have survived and become classics for the sole reason that, although they sought out new subjects, they never ceased to recognize the authority of the school. Actually, I can think of only one work, *Corinne,* which has earned immortal glory without being modeled after the ancients. But as you know, it is the exception that confirms the rule.

We must not forget that the French public is even more obstinate in its admirations than are authors in their principles. After all, the most classical-minded of authors would forswear Racine and Vergil tomorrow if experience proved to them just once that this was the way to acquire genius. You express regret that *Macbeth* is not performed. It was performed, and the public did not want any part of it. It is of course true that they did not see the witches' sabbath; or the spectacle of two great armies clashing, jostling, and scuffling on the stage, as in melodrama; or, finally, Macduff bringing in the head of Macbeth.

There you have the substance of my doctrine or my prejudices. This does not prevent the *romantics* from going their own way. But it would be well, I think, if a writer as positive and perceptive as yourself would be kind enough to show us what *the romantic* is in French literature—or rather, what it may be—relative to the taste that the latter has formed. I quite share your dislike for false grandeur, the jargon of literary coteries, and *marquis* wearing periwigs worth a thousand *écus.*[3] I agree with you that after one hundred and fifty years of the Académie Française, we are all terribly bored. But is it not true that what was good and beautiful in the ancients belongs to all times? Moreover, you say that today we need "a style that is clear, vivid, simple, and goes straight

[3] Cf. the Preface to the first part of *Racine and Shakespeare,* Bossange, 1823.

to the point." It seems to me that this is one of the rules of the classicists; and it is precisely what we are asking of MM. Nodier, Lamartine, Guiraud, Hugo, de Vigny, and associates.

As you can see, sir, we understand each other much better than one would have thought at first, and essentially we are fighting under almost the same banner. Please forgive my fulsomeness, and accept the expression of my most distinguished sentiments.[4]

Le C. N.

[4] The *Pandore* for March 29, 1824, says insultingly what the letter I have just transcribed says with great politeness and intelligence.

"What is *Romanticism?* Can one create a separate genre out of extravagance, disorder, and unreal enthusiasm? What does this puerile distinction mean? Essentially, there is neither a classic genre nor a romantic genre. . . . Let us be candid: this division that some people are trying to introduce into literature is the work of the mediocre. Are you endowed with well-balanced judgment? . . . Are you inclined toward overexcitement? . . . Be clear and elegant, and you will be sure not to find yourself in the company of those who have invented this *absurd distinction.*

E. Jouy"

I admit that several of the words employed by M. E. Jouy are not the kind I ordinarily use; but then I do not have to defend *Sylla.*

The Romantic to the Classicist

April 26

SIR,

If a man comes to someone and says, "I have an excellent method for making fine things," one says to him, "Go ahead and do it."

But if the man who comes is a surgeon named Forlenze; if he is talking to persons who were born blind; and if he tells them, by way of persuading them to submit to an operation for cataracts, "After the operation you will see beautiful things; for example, the sun . . ." they will interrupt him noisily. "Just show us any one person here," they will say, "who has seen the sun."

I have no intention of stretching this little analogy too far. But after all, no one in France has yet produced any work based on the romantic system—least of all those nice old gentlemen, Guiraud and associates. How, then, can I cite any examples for you?

I certainly do not deny that one can create fine things, even today, by following the *classical* system. But they will be boring.

This is because they will be partially based on the requirements of the French of 1670, and not on the moral needs and dominant passions of the Frenchman of 1824. *Pinto* is the only thing I can think of that was written for modern Frenchmen. If the police would allow *Pinto* to be performed, in less than six months the public would no longer be able to put up with conspiracies in alexandrine verse. And so I advise the classicists to have a tender regard for the police. Otherwise, they will be ingrates.

As for me, in my little sphere, at an immense distance from *Pinto* or any other work approved by the public, I will confess first of all that since 1814, for want of more serious pursuits, I have been writing much as one smokes a cigar—in order to pass the time. A page I have enjoyed writing is always good, for me.

And so, you see, I appreciate fully as much as I should, and more than anyone else, the great distance which separates me from those writers admired by the public and by the Académie Française. But if M. Villemain or M. de Jouy had received in the mails the manuscript of my *Vie de Rossini*,[1] they would have considered it "a piece of writing in a foreign language," and they would have translated it into beautiful academic style in the manner of the Preface to *La République de Cicéron*, by M. Villemain, or the letters of *Stephanus Ancestor*. An excellent venture for the publisher, who would have profited from twenty articles in the newspapers, and would by now be busy preparing the sixth edition of the book. But as for me, I would have become bored trying to write in the beautiful academic style; and I will confess that I would have played the role of a dupe. In my opinion, this contrived and formal style, full of pungent concluding phrases—and *precious,* if I must be quite frank—was marvelously appropriate for the Frenchmen of 1785. M. Delille was the hero of this style. I have *tried* to make mine suitable for the children of the Revolution; for people who are more interested in the idea than the beauty of the words; for people who, instead of reading Quintus Curtius or Tacitus, took part in the Moscow campaign and saw at first hand the strange transactions of 1814.

I have heard tell, in this age, of several little conspiracies. Since then I have come to scorn conspiracies in alexandrine verse and to wish for *tragedy in prose.* For example, a *Death of Henri III* of which the first four acts would take place in Paris and take up a month (that much time is required for the subordination of Jacques Clément) and the last act in Saint-Cloud. I confess that this would interest me more than Clytemnestra or Regulus delivering tirades of eighty lines,

[1] A copy of which, presumably, Stendhal had sent to the "classicist" friend with whom he is here corresponding. Cf. the second paragraph of the first letter. [Translator's note.]

and in the *official* spirit. The *tirade* is perhaps the most anti-romantic thing in the system of Racine. If it were absolutely necessary to choose, I would rather see the two unities preserved than the *tirade*.

You defy me, sir, to reply to the simple question: What is a romantic tragedy?

To this I reply boldly: It is a tragedy in prose that covers several months' time and takes place in various locales.

The poets who cannot understand this very difficult kind of discussion (M. Viennet, for example), and those people who do not want to understand, loudly demand a *clear* idea. Now it seems to me that nothing is clearer than the following: *A romantic tragedy is written in prose; the succession of events that it exhibits for the audience covers a period of several months; and the events take place in various locales.* May Heaven please send us soon a man of talent to write such a tragedy. Let him give us a *Death of Henri IV*, or *Louis XIII at Susa*. Then we shall see the brilliant Bassompierre as he says to that king—a true Frenchman, so brave and so weak: "Sire, the dancers are ready. When Your Majesty so desires, the dance will begin." [2]

---

[2] Everyone knows that Louis XIII, having experienced a fit of jealousy against his brother, Gaston, the duc d'Orléans, whom he had sent to command his army in Italy, hurried there himself and forced the Pass of Susa (1629). The danger was great, and the son of Henri IV showed his contempt for danger. Never did the French impetuosity make such a fine showing. The typical thing about this brilliant action was the total lack of tragic and melancholy rhetoric before the attack. Success was by no means certain. It was necessary to take, by sheer strength, well palisaded batteries that entirely barred the narrow valley coming down from Mount Cenis to Susa. It was either do this or go back to France. At such a decisive moment, Germans or Englishmen would not have failed to talk about God and grow melancholy, thinking of death and perhaps of Hell. What I like in my compatriots is the lack of such bombast.

Let us now suppose that a poet had the bad taste to want to give us an image of Louis XIII, Cardinal Richelieu, and the Frenchmen of their day, preferring modern subjects to Numa, Sesostris, Theseus, or some other hero very well known and even more interesting. I maintain that all this is impossible in alexan-

Our history—or rather, our historical memoirs, since we do not have any [written] history—is full of these fresh and charming sayings; and only romantic tragedy can make them

---

drine verse. All the nuances of character would disappear under the obligatory bombast of the alexandrine line.

It should also be remarked, in passing, that there is nothing less pompous and more natural than the true French character.

Here are the facts. Just before the attack on the Pass of Susa—a daring attack of very doubtful prospect—the Maréchal de Bassompierre, having positioned the attacking columns, came up to the king for the word of command. The dialogue was as follows:

"I approached the king (who was well out in front of the columns) and said to him: 'Sire, the company is ready, the violin players have entered, and the mummers are at the door. When Your Majesty so desires, we shall give the ballet.' He came up to me and said in anger: 'Do you know that we have only five hundred *livres* of shot in the artillery park?' I said to him: 'It is hardly the time to think of that now! Must the ballet be put off merely because one of the mummers is not ready? Let us proceed, Sire, and everything will go well.' 'Can I take your word for it?' he asked me. 'It would be foolhardy of me,' I replied, 'to guarantee such a doubtful thing. But I will assure you that either we shall come out of it honorably, or I will be dead or taken prisoner.' Then the cardinal said to him: 'Sire, to judge from the mien of M. le Maréchal, everything will go well, you can be assured.' At this, I dismounted and gave the signal for the battle, which was hard-fought and bloody, and which is a rather famous one." (*Mémoires de Bassompierre,* Part III, p. 192, Foucauld edition.)

This is the French character; this is the tone of our history. It is something you can never put into alexandrine verse. Instead, you will write a fine tirade, full of sense, for the Maréchal de Bassompierre; another tirade, full of high policy, for Louis XIII; and a *demi-vers,* full of character, for the famous cardinal. All this will be very fine, if you wish, but it will not be the history of France.

The Gascon naturalness shines through all the history of Henri IV, so little known in our day. It is in moments of great danger that the French sense of humor likes to show itself. The Frenchman, when he is in the smoke of musketry fire, believes he has the right to joke with his master. By means of such familiarity he shows his distinguished rank and then goes off, quite happy, to get himself killed.

It is perhaps amusing that we have chosen a mask that conceals precisely the most national, and perhaps the most amiable, trait in our character. The bombast of the alexandrine is suitable for

130

live for us again.[3] Do you know what would be the result if we had a romantic tragedy, in the manner of Shakespeare's *Richard III,* on the subject of Henri IV? Everybody would immediately agree on what is meant by the *romantic genre.* And before long, in the classic genre it would be impossible to perform anything except the plays of Corneille, of Racine, and of that Voltaire who found it was easier to use a completely epic style in *Mahomet, Alzire,* etc., than to keep to the noble and often very moving simplicity of Racine.

In 1670, a duke and peer attached to the court of Louis XIV, when he spoke to his son would address him as *Monsieur le marquis.* There was good reason why Racine had Pylades address Orestes as *Seigneur.* Today, fathers use the familiar form of *tu* when speaking to their children; and it would be *classical* to imitate the formalism in the dialogue of Pylades and Orestes. Today a friendship like theirs seems to us to require the use of *tu.*

But if I dare not explain what a romantic tragedy entitled the *Death of Henri IV* would be like, I can, on the other hand, quite freely give you an idea of a possible *romantic comedy* in five acts entitled *Lanfranc, or the Poet.* Here I run no other risk than that of boring you.

LANFRANC, OR THE POET
A Comedy in Five Acts

In the first act, Lanfranc the poet, with all the naïveté of a genius, goes to the Rue de Richelieu and presents his new

---

Protestants, for Englishmen, and even to some extent for the Romans; but it is certainly not suitable for the companions of Henri IV and Francis I.

[3] See, in the second volume of Froissart's *Chroniques,* published by M. Buchon, the account of the siege of Calais by Edward III and the devotedness of Eustache de Saint-Pierre. Immediately afterward, read *Le Siège de Calais,* a tragedy by du Belloy; and if Heaven has granted you any sensitivity of soul, you will passionately desire, as I do, *tragedy on national themes written in prose.* If the *Pandore* had not spoiled the word, I would say that this would be a genre eminently *French,* because no nation has memoirs on its medieval period that are so pungent as ours. The thing in Shakespeare that one should imitate is his *art,* his manner of depiction, and not the subjects depicted.

131

comedy to the committee of the Théâtre-Français. (As you can see, I am assuming that M. Lanfranc has genius. I fear the applications.) His comedy is rejected, as well it should have been, and they even laugh at him. After all, what man in Paris amounts to anything—even in literature—if he can't make advance sales of two hundred tickets for New Year's Day?

In the second act, Lanfranc starts to intrigue, because certain rash friends have advised him to intrigue. The first thing in the morning, he goes to see powerful people. But he intrigues with all the awkwardness of a genius; and his talk frightens the important people from whom he is seeking favors.

The result of his visits in the Faubourg Saint-Germain is that they throw him out as a dangerous madman at the very moment when he imagines he has won all the women's hearts by the charm of his imagination, and conquered all of the men by the profundity of his insights.

In the third act, because of all his troubles and disappointments, and above all, his unspeakable disgust at the idea of spending his life among people who care for nothing in the world but money and cordons, he is all ready to burn his comedy. But while intriguing, he has fallen passionately in love with a pretty actress from the Théâtre-Français, who returns his affections most tenderly.

The infinitely ridiculous spectacle of a man of genius in love with a Frenchwoman fills up the third act and a part of the fourth. In the middle of the fourth act, his beautiful mistress develops a preference for a young Englishman, a relative of Sir John Bikerstaff, who has only three millions of income. In order to recover from his pique, one night when he is in a state of despair, Lanfranc writes a pamphlet, fiery and full of verve, on the vexations and ridicule he has met with in the past two months. (This pamphlet is the comedy of the age.) But this verve and rage are so much *poison,* as Paul-Louis Courier says; and this poison leads him straight to the prison of Sainte-Pélagie.

The first fears of the indictment, the long faces of those liberal friends who were so brave the day before, the seizure of the pamphlet, the despair of the publisher (the father of seven children), the trial, the speech for the prosecution made by King's counsel, the moving speech for the defense made by M. Mérilhou, the ideas and jokes of the young lawyers present in the courtroom, and the strange things revealed by these remarks before, during, and after the verdict—there you have the fifth act. Its last scene shows us the poet sent to Sainte-Pélagie for fifteen days' imprisonment, followed by the loss of any hope that the censors will ever tolerate the performance of his comedies.

Well! after the seizure of *Les Tablettes romaines,* which occurred this morning, do you believe that I could have sketched out in this much detail a tragedy on the *Death of Henri IV,* an event of yesterday which is only two hundred and fourteen years old? And can you not see me, as a reward for my sketch, starting out the way my hero, Lanfranc, ended up?

That is what I call a romantic comedy. The events cover three and one-half months. They take place in different parts of Paris between the Théâtre-Français and the Rue de la Clef. And, finally, the comedy is in prose—in *ignoble prose,* believe it or not.

This comedy, *Lanfranc, or the Poet,* is romantic for another reason much more important than all those I have just cited but, I must admit, also much more difficult to grasp—so difficult that I almost hesitate to tell you. Those men of wit who have had success with tragedies written in verse will say that I am *obscure.* They have their own good reasons for not understanding. If *Macbeth* is performed in prose, what will happen to the fame of *Sylla?*

Lanfranc, or the Poet is a romantic comedy because the events *resemble* what takes place under our very eyes every day. The authors, the *grands seigneurs,* the judges, the lawyers, the literary men of the treasury, the spies, etc., who speak and act in this comedy are just as we see them every day in the salons. They are no more affected, no more pretentious, than in reality—and that is certainly enough. The

133

characters in classical comedy, on the contrary, seem to be wearing a double mask: first, the frightful affectation that we are obliged to put on in society, because otherwise we might not be properly esteemed; and then the affectation of nobility—something even more ridiculous—that the poet bestows upon them out of his own head by translating them into alexandrine verse.

Compare the events of the comedy entitled *Lanfranc, or the Poet* with the story of the same subject treated by the classical Muse (because from the first word, you will have guessed that I had a definite aim in choosing the leading character from one of the most famous classical comedies). Compare, I say, the behavior of Lanfranc to that of Damis in *La Métromanie*. There is no danger that I shall discuss the delightful style of that masterpiece, and for good reason. The comedy, *Lanfranc, or the Poet, has no style*. And in my opinion, that is where it shines. It is for that that I esteem it. It would be futile to look for a brilliant tirade in it. Only once or twice in the entire five acts does a character speak more than twelve or fifteen lines in succession. It is not the words of Lanfranc that cause astonishment and laughter. It is his deeds, prompted by motives that are not those of most men. And that is why he is a poet. Otherwise, he would be a man of letters.

Is there any need to add that what I have just said about the comedy of *Lanfranc* in no way proves that it shows talent? Now, if this play lacks fire and genius, it will be much more boring than a classical comedy, which, even if it offers no dramatic pleasure, does give us the pleasure of *hearing beautiful lines of poetry*. A romantic comedy without talent and having no beautiful lines to dazzle the spectator will bore people from the very first day.

And so we have returned by another path to that truth which is in such bad taste (so say the gentlemen of the Academy; or at any rate they pretend to): *The alexandrine line is often only a means of concealing stupidity.*[4]

[4] English or Italian verse can say anything; and it offers no obstacle to dramatic values.

But, assuming the talent is there, if the details of the comedy of *Lanfranc* are accurate, if it has fire, if the style never calls attention to itself, and if it resembles our everyday way of talking, then I say that this comedy meets the present needs of French society.

Molière, in *Le Misanthrope*, has a hundred times more genius than anyone else. But in an age when the *Miroir* can freely criticize the *Voyage à Coblentz*, Alceste not daring to tell the *marquis*, Oronte, that his sonnet is bad, exhibits to that giant called the Public (who is so terrifying and yet such a big booby) nothing more or less than the detailed portrait of something it has never seen and never will see.

After having had a glimpse of the comedy *Lanfranc, or the Poet*, which in order to establish my line of reasoning I must assume to be as good as the *Proverbes* of M. Théodore Leclercq, which so well depicts our actresses, our *grands seigneurs*, our judges, our liberal friends, Sainte-Pélagie, etc., etc.—in a word, society as it functions in 1824—please be so kind, sir, as to take another look at *La Métromanie*, the role of Francaleu, of the municipal officer, etc. And if, after having given yourself the pleasure of rereading those pretty verses, you declare that you prefer Damis to Lanfranc, what can I say in reply?

There are things one simply cannot prove. A man goes to see Raphael's "Transfiguration" at the Musée.[5] He turns toward me and says, with an expression of irritation: "I cannot see what is so sublime in this much-vaunted picture." "By the way," I say to him, "do you know what the rate on Government bonds was when the market closed yesterday?" Because it seems to me that when one meets people so very different from oneself, it is dangerous to get into a discussion. This is not pride, merely a fear of boredom. In Philadelphia, across the street from the house formerly occupied by Franklin, a Negro and a white man one day had a lively argument on the accuracy of Titian's color tones. Who was right? As a matter of fact, I don't know. But what I do know is that I

[5] It will be returned. (I.e., from the Vatican, to which the painting had been restituted in 1815. [Translator's note.])

and the man who does not like Raphael belong to two different species. There can be nothing in common between us. And I have not the slightest word to add to that fact.

A certain man has just read Racine's *Iphigénie en Aulide* and Schiller's *William Tell*. He swears to me that he prefers Achilles' boasts to the *antique* and truly great character of Tell. What is the purpose of arguing with such a man? I ask him how old his son is; and to myself I calculate when that son will make his appearance in society and mould public opinion.

If I were foolish enough to say to that good man, "Sir, give yourself a new experience: go to see just one performance of Schiller's *William Tell*," he would not hesitate to answer me like the true classicist of the *Journal des débats:* "Not only will I never go to see that coarse Teutonic rhapsody and never read it, but what is more, I will make sure through my own influence that it is never performed." [6]

Well! That classicist of the *Débats* who tries to combat an idea with a bayonette is not so ridiculous as he seems. Although most men are unaware of it, habit exercises a despotic power over their imaginations. I could cite the example of a great king, very well educated, moreover, and the kind of person one would think was quite free of illusions about sensitivity. That king cannot bear to have a man of worth present at his council if the man in question does not powder his hair. An unpowdered head of hair evokes for him the bloody images of the French Revolution—the first things forcibly to strike his royal imagination, thirty years ago. A man with his hair cut short, like us, could submit to that king projects conceived with the profundity of Richelieu or the prudence of Kaunitz; and during the whole time he was reading them, the king would pay attention only to the repulsive haircut of the cabinet minister.

I see a gem of literary tolerance in this story: habit exercises a despotic power over the imaginations of even the most enlightened men and, through their imaginations, over the pleasures that the arts can bring to them. How can one

[6] An actual quotation.

find the secret of separating such aversions from the wit of those amiable Frenchmen who cut such a brilliant figure at the court of Louis XVI, whom M. de Ségur has brought back to life in his charming reminiscences, and whose ideas of elegance are described as follows in the *Masque de Fer:*

I was telling myself how, in the old days (that is, in 1786), if I had to go to the Chamber, and if, desirous of getting a little exercise for my health, I left my carriage at the Pont Tournant intending to enter it again at the Pont Royal, my costume alone would recommend me to the respect of the public. I would be wearing what we called so ridiculously a *habit habillé*. This costume was of velvet or satin in winter and taffeta in the summer. It was embroidered and decorated with my orders. However strongly the wind was blowing, I would have my plumed hat under my arm. I would be wearing a toupee, square-shaped, with five points standing out on my forehead. I would be powdered to the point of hoarfrost, with white powder on top of gray powder. My coiffure would be set off by a row of ringlets on each side, and in the back by a beautiful *bourse* of black taffeta. I agree with Your Highness that this coiffure is not primitive; but it is eminently aristocratic and, consequently, social. However cold it was, with frost and a freezing wind, I would cross the Tuileries in stockings of white silk and shoes of kidskin. A small sword—decorated with ribbons and a sword-knot, because I was a colonel at the age of eighteen—would slap against my leg. My hands, adorned with long lace sleeves, would be hidden in a muff of blue fox-skin. A light *douillette* of taffeta, simply tossed over my person, would create the impression of protecting me against the cold; and I would believe it myself.[7]

I am very much afraid that in music, painting, and tragedy, we and those Frenchmen will always remain unintelligible to one another.

There are classicists who, without knowing Greek, lock

[7] *Le Masque de Fer,* p. 150.

themselves in their rooms to read Homer in French; and even in French they think the great painter of savage times is sublime. But just let the word TRAGEDY be printed above the lifelike and impassioned dialogues that are the most engaging part of Homer's poetry, and immediately these dialogues, which those gentlemen had admired as epic poetry, will be shocking and mortally displeasing to them as tragedy. This repugnance is absurd; but they have no control over it. Yet they feel it, and they take it for granted, just as we take for granted the tears we shed at *Romeo and Juliet*. I can see how, for these estimable men of letters, romanticism is an insolence. They have enjoyed unanimity for forty years, and then you warn them that soon they will be alone in their opinion.

If prose tragedy were a physical necessity of human beings, one could undertake to demonstrate its utility to them. But how does one prove to a person that a thing which arouses an overwhelming feeling of repugnance in him can and should give him pleasure?

I have the utmost respect for classicists of this sort, and I pity them for having been born in an age when sons are so little like their fathers. What a change there was between 1785 and 1824! There has probably never been such an abrupt revolution in habits, ideas, and beliefs in the two thousand years since we have known the history of the world. One of the friends of my family, to whose country home I had gone to pay my respects, was saying to his son: "What is the meaning of your eternal solicitations and your bitter complaints against the minister of war? You are already a lieutenant of cavalry at thirty-three. Do you realize that I was not made a captain until I was fifty?"

The son was flushed with anger. And yet the father had said something that, for him, was altogether obvious. How could this father and son be made to agree with each other?

How can one persuade a fifty-year-old man of letters who finds brilliantly natural the role of Zamore in *Alzire*, that Shakespeare's *Macbeth* is one of the masterpieces of the human mind? I was saying one day to a gentleman of this type: "Twenty-eight million people—that is, eighteen million in England and ten million in America—admire and applaud

Macbeth a hundred times a year." "The English," he replied with great equanimity, "cannot have either genuine eloquence or truly admirable poetry. The nature of their language, which is not derived from Latin, makes this quite impossible." What can one say to such a man—who incidentally is a person of very good will. We are still at the same point: How *prove* to someone that the "Transfiguration" is admirable?

Molière was romantic in 1670, because the court was full of Orontes and the châteaux in the provinces were full of very discontented Alcestes. Actually, ALL GREAT WRITERS WERE THE ROMANTICS OF THEIR DAY. The classicists are those who, a century after the death of the great writers, copy them instead of opening their eyes and imitating nature.[8]

Are you interested in observing the effect produced on the stage by this circumstance of *resembling nature* added to a masterpiece? Consider the rapid rise in the success of *Le Tartuffe* in the past four years. Under the Consulate and during the first years of the Empire, *Le Tartuffe* resembled nothing in this world, like *Le Misanthrope*. But this did not prevent the Laharpes, the Lemerciers, the Augers, and the other great critics from exclaiming, *"A picture of all times and of all places,"* etc., or the provincials from applauding.

The height of absurdity, and of classicism, is to see costumes adorned with gold lace in most of our modern comedies. The authors are only too right: the falsity of the costume prepares one for the falsity of the dialogue. And just as the alexandrine is very useful for the would-be poet devoid of ideas, so the costume with gold lace is no less useful for the

---

[8] Vergil, Tasso, and Terence are perhaps the only great *classical* poets. Tasso still makes constant use of classical forms copied from Homer to express the tender and chivalrous sentiments of his own age. At the time of the literary renaissance, after the barbarism of the ninth and tenth centuries, Vergil was so superior to the poem of the Abbé Abbon on the siege of Paris by the Normans, that, however slight one's sensitivity, it was impossible not to be a classicist and prefer Turnus to Hérivée. In the same way as those things which now seem most odious to us— feudalism, the monks, etc.—classicism had its day when it was useful and natural. But today (February 15, the day of Mardi gras) is it not ridiculous that the only *farce* offered for my amusement is *Pourceaugnac,* written a hundred and fifty years ago?

embarrassed demeanor and conventional charms of the poor, untalented actor.

Monrose plays Crispins[9] very well; but who ever saw a Crispin?

Perlet, and Perlet alone, gave us a lifelike portrayal of the ridiculous traits in our present-day society. He showed us, for example, the *glumness* of our young men, who upon graduation from school, begin life so intellectually, with all the seriousness of a man of forty. What happened? One evening Perlet refused to imitate the servility of the bad actors of 1780; and because he behaved like a Frenchman of 1824, all the theatres are closed to him.

I have the honor, etc.

S.

[9] The name conventionally given to the stock character of the valet and jester in old French comedy. [Translator's note.]

The Romantic to the Classicist

April 26, Noon

SIR,

Your inexorable sagacity inspires me with fear. I am taking up the pen again, two hours after having written to you. Now that the mails are so fast, I tremble in anticipation of your reply. The admirable precision of your mind will enable you to attack me, I am sure, through a side door that I left open to criticism. Alas! My intention was praiseworthy: I was trying to be brief.

Romanticism, as applied to those pleasures of the mind with regard to which the real battle between the classicists and the romantics—between Racine and Shakespeare—is taking place, means a prose tragedy which covers several months and whose events take place in various locales. There may, however, be a romantic tragedy whose events are confined, purely by chance, to the locale of a palace and a duration of thirty-six hours. If the different incidents of this tragedy resemble those unveiled to us by history, and if the diction, instead of being epic and official, is simple, lively, strikingly natural, and without tirades, the accident which caused the events of this tragedy to take place in a palace and within the period of time indicated by the Abbé d'Aubignac will not prevent it from being romantic; that is, from offering the public the impressions it needs and, consequently, winning the votes of those who think for themselves. Shakespeare's *Tempest*, however mediocre it may be, is nonetheless a romantic play, although it covers only a few hours and the events composing it take place on, and in the immediate vicinity of, a little island in the Mediterranean.

You combat my theories, sir, by recalling the success of several tragedies modeled after Racine (*Clytemnestre, Le*

141

Paria, etc.); that is, tragedies that more or less awkwardly meet, today, the requirements imposed upon Racine by the taste of the *marquis* of 1670 and the court of Louis XIV. To which I reply: So great is the power of dramatic art over the human heart that, however absurd the rules to which the poor poets must submit, that art still manages to please. If Aristotle or the Abbé d'Aubignac had imposed upon French tragedy the rule that characters should speak only in words of one syllable—if every word of more than one syllable were banished from the French stage and from poetic style with the same severity as the word *pistolet,* for example—well, I say that despite this absurd rule, tragedies written by men of genius would still give pleasure. Why? Because notwithstanding the rule of the monosyllable (no more astounding than many others), the man of genius would have found a way to put into his play a wealth of thought and abundance of feeling that claim our attention from the start. The stupidity of the rule would have compelled him to sacrifice several poignant lines and several sentiments of sure effect. But this matters little to the success of his tragedy *so long as the rule exists.* It is when the rule finally crumbles under the belated blows delivered by good sense, that the old poet runs a real risk. *With much less talent,* his successors will be able to surpass him in the same subject. Why? Because they will dare to use the right, unique, necessary, *indispensable* word to express a certain emotion or to tell of some incident in the plot. How is it possible for Othello, for example, not to say the ignoble word "handkerchief" when he is killing the woman he adores, solely because she allowed his rival, Cassio, to get hold of the fatal handkerchief that he had given her during the first days of their love.

If the Abbé d'Aubignac had ruled that actors in *comedy* could only hop about on one leg, Marivaux's comedy, *Les Fausses confidences,* with Mademoiselle Mars performing, would still stir our emotions despite such a bizarre idea. We simply would not see the bizarre idea.[1] Our grandfathers were deeply moved by the Orestes of *Andromaque* played

[1] In the arts, an absurdity that is not noticed does not exist.

by an actor wearing a great powdered wig, red stockings, and shoes with flame-colored ribbon tied into bow-knots.

Any absurdity to which the imagination of a people has become accustomed is no longer an absurdity for them; and it interferes hardly at all with the pleasures of the great mass of the people, until the fatal moment when some indiscreet individual says: "What you admire is absurd." When this phrase is spoken, many persons who are sincere with themselves and had believed that their souls were insensitive to poetry, begin to breathe freely. Because they had loved it too much, they thought they didn't love it at all. Similarly, a young man whom Heaven has endowed with a certain degree of sensitivity, if chance makes him a second lieutenant and puts him in a garrison, in the society of certain women, will believe most sincerely, when he sees the success of his comrades and the kind of pleasures they enjoy, that he is insensitive to love. But one day, chance finally causes him to meet a woman who is simple, natural, honest, and worthy of being loved; and he realizes that he does have a heart.

Many older persons are classicists in good faith. First of all, they do not understand the word "romantic." Everything that is lugubrious and silly, like the seduction of Eloa[2] by Satan, they believe to be romantic, on the say-so of the *poètes-associés des bonnes lettres*. The contemporaries of Laharpe admire the slow and lugubrious tone that Talma still uses too often in the tirades. This lamentable and monotonous chant they call "the perfection of French tragedy." [3] They say (and it is a poor argument): "The use of prose in tragedy, and allowing the action to cover several months and to take place at locales several leagues apart, is of no use to our pleasures. Because very moving masterpieces have been written and are still being written with scrupulous adherence to the rules of the Abbé d'Aubignac." To this we reply: "Our tragedies would be even more moving; and they would deal with a great many national themes that Voltaire and Racine had to avoid." The art will undergo a change of aspect as soon as

[2] In Alfred de Vigny's poem of the same name. [Translator's note.]
[3] *Le Journal des débats for* March 30, 1823.

143

it is permissible to change the stage setting. For example, to move from Paris to Saint-Cloud in a tragedy about the death of Henri III.

Now that I have explained myself at great length, it seems to me that I may say, with the hope of being understood by everybody and the assurance that I will not be parodied, even by the *renowned* M. Villemain:[4] Romanticism as applied to the tragic genre IS A TRAGEDY IN PROSE THAT COVERS SEVERAL MONTHS AND TAKES IN VARIOUS LOCALES.

When the Romans built those monuments that still compel our admiration after so many centuries (Septimus Severus' Arch of Triumph, Constantine's Arch of Triumph, the Arch of Titus, etc.), what they carved on the surfaces of those famous arches were soldiers armed with shields, helmets, and swords. Nothing could have been simpler: those were the arms with which their soldiers had recently conquered the Germans, the Parthians, the Jews, etc.

When Louis XIV had erected in his honor that arch of triumph known as the Porte Saint-Martin, French soldiers attacking the walls of a city were carved in bas-relief on the side of the arch that faces to the north. Those soldiers are armed with shields and helmets and wear coats of mail. Now I ask you: Did the soldiers of Turenne and of the great Condé, who won Louis XIV's battles for him, go armed with shields? What good is a shield against a cannon ball? Was Turenne killed by a javelin?

The Roman artists were *romantics:* they depicted that which, in their time, was true—and hence emotionally stirring for their fellow countrymen.

Louis XIV's sculptors were *classicists:* in the bas-reliefs of their arch of triumph (well deserving of the ignoble name of Porte Saint-Martin) they exhibited figures that do not resemble anything seen in their day.

To those young men who have not yet had a tragedy accepted by the Théâtre-Français, and who therefore put some good faith into this frivolous debate, I address the following

---

[4] *Le Journal des débats,* March 30, 1823.

question. After an example so clear, so tangible (and so easy to verify some day when you go to see Mazurier) can one say to the romantics that they do not know how to explain themselves—that they do not give a very clear idea of what it means, in the arts, to be romantic or classical? I do not ask you, gentlemen, to say that my idea is correct. I merely want you to acknowledge that, whether it be good or bad, you understand it.

I am, etc.

Letter IV

The Classicist to the Romantic

Paris, April 27, 1824

SIR,

For almost sixty years, now, I have admired *Mérope, Zaïre, Iphigénie, Sémiramis,* and *Alzire*;[1] and in good conscience I cannot promise you that I will ever hiss these masterpieces of the human mind. I am nonetheless quite ready to applaud the prose tragedies that the romantic Messiah is supposed to bring us. But we have already been waiting for a long time, and your Messiah has not yet appeared. *Do something, sir; do something.* The mere words of literary men (always obscure for the common people, anyway) are no longer of any use to your faction: deeds are what it must now produce. So let us have some of them, sir, and *we shall see how things turn out.*

Meantime (and I believe it will be a considerable time), please accept the assurance of my most distinguished sentiments, etc. etc.

Le C. N.[2]

[1] With the exception of *Iphigénie (en Aulide),* all these plays are by Voltaire. [Translator's note.]

[2] This exchange of letters actually took place. However, I was understating the case to a man of good faith. In preparing my letters for publication, I was obliged to explain everything clearly. Otherwise, MM. Auger, Feletz, and Villemain would have attributed some fine absurdities to me.

Letter V

The Romantic to the Classicist

Paris, April 24 [28?], 1824

SIR,

Just a moment! Who ever suggested hissing Voltaire, Racine, or Molière, those immortal geniuses the likes of which our poor France may not see again for another eight or ten centuries? Who even dared to conceive the foolish hope that these great men might be equaled? They entered the race wearing chains. And they wore them so gracefully that certain pedants have managed to convince the French that heavy chains are an indispensable ornament to a runner.

There is the whole question. Because for [a hundred and] fifty years we have waited in vain for a genius the equal of Racine, we are requesting a public fond of watching races in an arena, to allow runners to perform without heavy chains. If this were done, several young poets of remarkable talent (although still far from possessing the astounding *strength* that is so striking in the masterpieces of Molière, Corneille, or Racine) could give us some enjoyable plays. Will you go on insisting that they wear the cumbersome armor once worn so gracefully by Racine and Voltaire? If so, they will go on giving you *well-made* plays like *Clytemnestre, Louis IX, Jeanne d'Arc,* and *Le Paria,* which in our day have succeeded Luce de Lancival's *Mort d'Hector,* Baour-Lormian's *Omasis,* and Legouvé's *Mort de Henri IV*—masterpieces whose faithful companions *Clytemnestre* and *Germanicus* will become just as soon as the authors of these tragedies are no longer there to prop up their reputations in the salons by their amiability, and in the newspapers by favorable articles.

I have no doubt, for example, but that my favorite tragedy about the death of Henri III will forever remain much inferior to *Britannicus* and the *Horaces*.[1] In *Henri III* the public will find much less—infinitely less—talent, and much more interest and dramatic pleasure. If Britannicus behaved in the real world as he does in Racine's tragedy, once he was stripped of the charm of the beautiful lines expressing his feelings, he would strike us as a bit foolish and a bit dull.

Racine could not deal with the death of Henri III. That heavy chain called the *unity of place* forever barred him from that great tableau—heroic and inflamed, like the passions of the Middle Ages, and yet so close to us, who are so cold. This was a piece of good luck for our young playwrights. If men like Corneille and Racine had had to meet the demands of the public of 1824, with its mistrust of everything, its complete lack of beliefs or passions, its habit of lying, its fear of being compromised, the gloomy melancholy of its young people, etc., etc., tragedy would be impossible to write for a century or two.

Endowed with the masterpieces of the great men who were contemporaries of Louis XIV, France will never forget them. I am convinced that the classical Muse will always occupy the Théâtre-Français four times a week. All we ask is that prose tragedy be permitted, five or six times a month, to entertain us with the great deeds of our Du Guesclins, our Montmorencys, and our Bayards. I confess that I would like to see, on the French stage, the *Death of the Duc de Guise at Blois*, or *Joan of Arc and the English*, or *the Assassination at the Pont de Montereau*. These great and calamitous scenes taken from our annals would strike a sensitive chord in the hearts of all Frenchmen and, according to the romantics, would interest them more than the misfortunes of Oedipus.

In speaking of drama, sir, you tell me, *"Do something!"* But you are forgetting the censors. Is this justice, Monsieur le Classique? Is this good faith? If I were to write a romantic comedy like *Pinto*, resembling what we see in the world around us, first, MM. the Censors would stop it; and second, the *liberal* students at the big colleges of law and medicine would hiss it. Because these young men acquire their opinions

---

[1] Presumably Corneille's *Horace*, based on the legend of the three brothers of this name. [Translator's note.]

148

ready-made in *Le Constitutionnel,* the *Courrier français,* or *Pandore.* Now, what would happen to the divers masterpieces of MM. Jouy, Dupaty, Arnault, Etienne, Gosse, etc.—the editors of those newspapers, and very clever editors—if Talma were ever allowed to perform *Macbeth* in prose, translated from Shakespeare and cut by one-third? It was just such such a fear that made those gentlemen hiss the English actors.

I have a remedy against the first evil, *censorship,* and I shall give it to you shortly. As for the bad taste of the students, I see no other remedy for this than pamphlets against Laharpe, and I am writing them.

On Censorship

All the comic poets to whom one says, "Do something," protest: "As soon as we put true details into our dramas, the censors stop us short. Just consider the scene the censors would not allow in *Le Cid d'Andalousie*—the one in which the king is given a beating with a cane." My reply is: "This reason is not so good as it seems to be. You submit to the censors things like *La Princesse des Ursins* and *Les Intrigues de cour*—very piquant comedies in which you mock the ridiculous traits of the court with the tact and wit of a Voltaire. [But why do you attack only the absurdities of the court?] This may be a good and laudable undertaking, politically speaking. But I maintain that literally speaking it is worth nothing. Suppose, for instance, that while we are laughing and joking with some charming women in a salon, someone comes in and says the house is on fire. That relaxed attention necessary for witticisms and the pleasures of the mind will be dissipated at once. Such is the effect produced by any political idea in a work of literature. It is like a pistol shot in the middle of a concert."

The least political allusion destroys the mood proper to all those subtle pleasures that are the object of the poet's efforts. This truth has been proved by the history of English literature. (And please note that the condition we are in has lasted in England since the Restoration of 1660.) Among our

English neighbors, men of the greatest talent have dealt the death blow to some very enjoyable works by introducing allusions to the transient but thorny political questions of the day. In order to understand Swift, one has to have a long and tedious commentary; and no one takes the trouble to read such a commentary. The soporific effect of politics mixed with literature is an axiom in England. This is the reason why Sir Walter Scott, although he is an ultraconservative and occupies the same position at Edinburgh that M. de Marchangy does at Paris, is very careful not to put politics into his novels. He is afraid that otherwise they would suffer the same fate as *La Gaule poétique*.

The instant you introduce politics into literature, *the odious* makes its appearance; and along with it, *impotent rage*. Now, once your heart has become a prey to impotent rage—that fatal illness of the nineteenth century—you no longer have enough good spirits left to laugh at anything. "A fine time to be laughing!" you would reply indignantly to the person who was trying to make you laugh.[2] The newspapers, witnesses of what took place in the elections of 1824, vie with one another in exclaiming: "What a fine subject for comedy in *L'Eligible!*" On the contrary, gentlemen, it is worth nothing. There would be the role of a prefect who would not make me laugh at all. Just look at the novel entitled *Monsieur le Préfet.* Is there anything more [true to life]? But then, is there anything more gloomy? Sir Walter Scott, in *Waverley,* avoided impotent rage by describing burning passions that today are only ashes.

Messieurs les poètes comiques, why do you attempt in your art the one thing that is impossible? Could it be that you are like those false heroes of the provincial cafes, who are never so ferocious as when they are seated around a table with their friends, telling tales of combat while everyone admires them?

Since M. de Chateaubriand defended religion as *pretty,* others, with greater success, have defended kings as useful to the happiness of nations—as necessary in our stage of civilization. The Frenchman does not spend his life at the forum as the Greek or Roman did. He considers even jury duty as a

[2] Translated from Hazlitt.

bother, etc. By means of this kind of defense, kings have been made into ordinary men. They are loved, but no longer worshiped. Madame du Hausset tells us that their mistresses laugh at them, just as ours laugh at us. And M. le duc de Choiseul, the prime minister, has made with M. de Praslin a certain bet I must not reveal.

Since the time when kings ceased to be regarded as beings *sent from on High*, like Philip II and Louis XIV; since the day when some insolent individual proved that they were *useful*—their worth has been subject to debate, and comedy has had forever to abandon its jokes about courtiers. Appointments as cabinet ministers are won on the rostrum at the Chamber of Deputies and not in the Oeil-de-Boeuf. And do you expect kings to tolerate jokes about their poor courts, which are already so deserted? In all truth, that is not reasonable. Would you advise them to do it if you were minister of police? Is it not true that the first law for any individual, be he wolf or sheep, is self-preservation? Any joke about the government may be very courageous, but it is not literature.

Today, the slightest joke about kings or the Holy Alliance, made on the stage of the Théâtre-Français, would be met with wild applause. Not, mind you, as a *good joke;* not as a witticism the equal of Harpagon's "No dowry" or "The poor man!" from *Le Tartuffe,* but as a startling breach of propriety—as a bit of boldness which would leave everyone astonished. They would be astonished by your courage, but it would be a poor success for your wit. Because just as soon as there is censorship in a country, the poorest joke about the government succeeds. M. Casimir Delavigne believes people applaud the wittiness of his *Comédiens,* whereas in fact they are often merely applauding the liberal opinions expressed in allusions that have eluded the vigilance of M. Lémontey.

I therefore say to the comic poets (if there are any with real talent who think they have the power to make us laugh): Satirize the ridiculous traits of the ordinary classes of society. Do you think deputy ministers are the only ridiculous people? Put on the stage that famous patriot who has devoted his life to the cause of the nation, who exists only for the happiness of humanity, and who lends his money to the King of Spain so that he can pay the hangman of R***. If queried about such a loan, he replies: "My heart is patriotic, as everyone well knows. But my *écus* are Royalist."

Does that ridiculous person aspire to esteem? Refuse him that esteem in a piquant and surprising manner, and you will be creating comedy. On the other hand, I find nothing particularly amusing in the pretentions of the reverend Jesuit fathers—most of them poor wretches born in poverty who are simply trying to live a comfortable life without doing manual labor.

Do you find it improper to dramatize the ridiculous traits of a patriot who, after all, is speaking in favor of a prudent kind of freedom and looking for ways to impart a bit of moral courage to voters who are so brave when they have sword in hand? Try imitating Alfieri.

Just imagine some fine day when all the censors are dead, and there is no more censorship; but, on the other hand, there are four or five theatres in Paris free to perform anything they want and responsible for objectionable things, improprieties, etc., only to a jury picked by chance.[3]

It was under just such a strange supposition that Alfieri, in a country run much more strictly than ours, and in a much more hopeless state, composed his admirable tragedies forty years ago. But they are performed every day; and a nation of eighteen million people, which has gallows instead of a prison like Sainte-Pélagie, knows them by heart and quotes them on every possible occasion. Editions of these tragedies sell widely in all formats; and when one of them is performed, the theatre is full two hours ahead of curtain time. In a word, the success of Alfieri is beyond anything that even the vanity of a poet could dream of; and this whole great change has taken place in less than twenty years. Write, then, and you will be applauded in 1845.

Will the present minister ban the comedy you are going to write for us today—one which will not portray the poor clerk, Bellemain, of *L'Interieur d'un bureau,* but instead M.

[3] From among those inhabitants of Paris who pay five thousand francs in taxes and are hence very moderate advocates of the agrarian law and of license.

le comte So-and-So, P[eer] o[f] F[rance]? If so, practice that precept of Horace that used to be so highly recommended (in another sense, it is true): Keep your play for nine years, and you will be dealing with another ministry, which will be trying to ridicule that of today and perhaps to scoff at it. Believe me: in nine years you will find all conditions favorable for having your comedy performed.

That charming bit of vaudeville, *Julien, ou Vingt-cinq Ans d'entr'acte,* can serve as an example for you. Of course it is only a sketch. But with respect to courage and censorship, that sketch is worth just as much, for the purpose of my argument, as the most substantial comedy in five acts. Would it have been possible to give a performance of this vaudeville sketch in 1811, under Napoleon? Just think of how M. Etienne and all the censors of the Imperial Police would have shuddered at the sight of the young peasant who had distinguished himself by the sword in the campaigns of the Revolution and had been made *Duc de Stettin* by His Majesty the Emperor, exclaiming, when his daughter wanted to marry a painter: "Never! Never has there been a misalliance in the family of the Stettins!" How would this have affected the vanity of all the counts of the Empire?

Would M. le duc de R*** have considered exile forty leagues away from Paris a sufficient punishment for the impudent fellow who took the liberty of saying such a thing?

Nonetheless, *Monsieur le poète comique,* if in that same year of 1811, instead of uttering monotonous and futile complaints about the arbitrary acts and despotism of Napoleon, etc., etc., etc., you had acted with speed and strength (as he himself acted), if you had written comedies which made people laugh at the absurdities that Napoleon was obliged to defend in order to maintain his *French Empire,* his *new nobility,* etc., they would have enjoyed a tremendous success less than four years later.

But, you will say, my satire may become dated with the passage of time.

Yes, like Harpagon's "No dowry" or "The poor man!" from *Le Tartuffe.* Are you seriously offering this objection to a public that still has nothing better to laugh at than the absurdities of Clitandre and Acaste,[4] which have not existed for the past hundred years?

If in 1811, instead of complaining peevishly about the insurmountable obstacles that the age puts in the way of poetry and envying Molière the sponsorship of Louis XIV, you had written great comedies as free in their political opinions as the vaudeville sketch, *Vingt-cinq Ans d'entr'acte,* would not all the theatres have offered you a special place in 1815? Think of the honors that would have been heaped upon you! In 1815, you understand? Only four years later. How joyously we would have laughed at the stupid vanity of the princes of the Empire![5] At first, you would have enjoyed a *succès de satire,* like Alfieri in Italy. Then little by little, when Napoleon's system was *completely dead,* you would have had the success of *Waverley* and *Old Mortality.* (Since the death of the last Stuart, is anyone really repulsed by the character of the Baron of Bradwardine, or the Major Bridgenorth of *Peveril?* In 1824, our politics of 1811 is merely history.)

If in accordance with the most rudimentary common sense, you write today without troubling about our present censorship, by 1834, out of a proper respect for yourself and in order to avoid the displeasure of any resemblance to the literary men on the payroll of the Treasury of that day, you may be obliged to soften the strokes in which you have depicted the evil absurdities of the powerful men of today.[6]

Are you impatient? Are you dead set on becoming popular with your contemporaries while you are still young? Is it fame that you need? Write your comedies as if you were exiled to New York. Not only that: have them published in New York under an assumed name. If they are sarcastic, disagreeable, and gloomy they will fail to cross the ocean and will fall into the deep oblivion that they deserve. (There is no lack of causes, today, for indignation and feelings of

[4] The *marquis* of *Le Misanthrope.*
[5] "Between the two of us, *'monseigneur'* is enough."
[6] "It was Monsieur So-and-So who conceived the happy idea of cutting off a man's hand." Or *"Monseigneur,* when you are not talking, why, I declare! I vote according to my conscience."

impotent hatred. Don't we have Colmar and Greece for that?) But if your comedies are good, pleasant, and amusing, like the *Lettre* on recreational government and *La Marmite représentative,* M. Demat, the honest printer of Brussels, will not fail to render you the same service that he has rendered to M. Béranger. Within three months he will have pirated your work in all possible formats. You will see it in all the bookstores of Europe. And the business men from Lyon who are going to Geneva will be asked by twenty different friends to bring back a copy of your comedy for them, just as today they are asked to bring back a copy of Béranger.[7]

But alas! I see from the frown on your face that my advice is only too good. It is putting you out of sorts. Your comedies have so little comic verve and so little warmth that no one would notice their wit, no one would laugh at the jokes in them, were it not for the fact that every day they are praised, recommended, and preached by the newspapers you work for. Of what use is it to talk to you of New York and an assumed name? You could publish your epistles in dialogue at Paris, and instead of being a sure path to Sainte-Pélagie for you, they would be a sure path to bankruptcy for your publisher. Or else he would die of grief, like the one who paid twelve thousand francs for *L'Histoire de Cromwell.*

Ungrateful wretches! Since this is the way things are, don't complain any more about that fine institution of censorship. It renders the greatest of services to your vanity. It enables you to convince others, and perhaps even yourselves, that you would do something if. . . .

You liberal and persecuted writers—without those fine gentlemen, the censors, your fate would be horrible. The Frenchman is born ready for humor. You would be flooded with things like *Le Mariage de Figaro* and *Pinto;* in short,

[7] The volume of this great poet which, thanks to M. Demat, costs three francs at Geneva, sells for twenty-four francs at Lyons, and no one buys it there. The most amusing thing at the customs house in Bellegarde, located between Geneva and Lyons, is the list of prohibited books posted in the office. As I was reading this list and laughing at its futility, several honest travelers were copying it so that they could bring in the books listed. All of them told me that they had brought in copies of Béranger to Lyons. March, 1824.

with comedies *that make people laugh.* I ask you: What would then happen to your lifeless plays that are so well written? You would play the same role in literature that M. Paer plays in music, now that Rossini has caused his operas to be forgotten. This is the whole secret of your great wrath against Shakespeare. What will happen to your tragedies when they start giving performances of *Macbeth* and *Othello*, as translated by Madame Belloc? Racine and Corneille, in whose names you speak, have nothing to fear from this juxtaposition. But you!

Do I hear you saying that I am an impudent fellow and you have genius? Fine, I admit it. Am I agreeable enough now? So, you have genius, like Béranger. But unlike him, you do not know how to do things modestly and reproduce in Paris the practical wisdom and sublime philosophy of the Greek philosophers. You need your writings in order to attain

To the superfluous, that thing so necessary.

Well, then! In that case, transform your comedies into novels by means of adding a few descriptions, and have them published in Paris. The people in high society, whose luxurious living during the winter exiles them to the country beginning in the month of May, have a tremendous need for novels. You would have to be very boring indeed to be more so than a family evening in the country when it is raining outside.[8]

I have the honor, etc.

[8] I have just received the fourth sheet of this brochure all besmeared with the fatal red ink. I must delete the fine *eulogy of the hangman,* by M. de Maistre, considered in its relation to comedy; the anecdote involving MM. de Choiseul and de Praslin; and, in short, everything that might offend the powerful ones. At first I said to myself: What a blessing it would be to live in Philadelphia! But little by little my thoughts grew calmer, and I arrived at the following considerations.

Constitutional government, considered in all its vigorous phases —in 1819 as in 1825—has three great defects as regards literature:

1) It takes away that leisure without which there are no fine arts. Italy, in gaining its two legislative chambers, may perhaps lose its Canovas and Rossinis.

2) It fills all hearts with argumentative defiance. It separates the different classes of citizens by hate. (When you meet a man socially in Dijon or Toulouse, you no longer ask: What is his ridiculous trait? Instead, you ask: Is he liberal or conservative?) It takes away from the different classes of citizens the desire to be amiable in the eyes of one another and, consequently, the capacity for laughing at the expense of one another.

An Englishman traveling on the coach to Bath is careful not to talk or joke about the most indifferent thing in the world. It might develop that the man next to him is of an enemy class: a Methodist or a bilious Tory who will send him about his business. Because anger is a pleasure for the English: it makes them aware of living. How can *subtlety of wit* ever develop in a country where one can publish with impunity the phrase, *"George is a libertine,"* and where only the word *"king"* constitutes the offense? In a country like this, only two sources of humor are left: false heroes and cuckolded husbands; and a ridiculous trait is called "eccentricity."

The true homeland of comedy is a despotism without too many gallows. In France under Louis XIV and Louis XV, everyone traveling by coach had the same interests, laughed at the same things and, what is more, wanted to laugh, since they were removed from the serious interests of life.

3) They say that the inhabitants of that Philadelphia I was longing for think only of earning dollars and scarcely know what the word "ridiculous" means. *Laughter* is an exotic plant imported from Europe at great expense and available only to the richest people. (The voyage of the actor, Mathews.) The lack of subtlety, added to the Puritanical pedantry, makes the comedy of Aristophanes impossible in that republic.

None of the foregoing prevents justice, liberty, and the absence of spies from being benefits worthy of adoration. *Laughter* is merely a consolation employed by the subjects of monarchy. But just as the oyster produces the pearl, so men without liberty, *and without a Christian burial* after their death, produce *Le Tartuffe* and *Le Retour imprévu.*

I have never in my life talked to a censor; but I imagine that one of them might say, by way of justifying his profession:

Even if all France were unanimously in favor of it, we could never recreate the men of 1780. The admirable libretto of *Don Giovanni,* set to music by Mozart, was written in Vienna by the Abbé Casti [Giovanni Battista Casti, Italian poet, a contemporary (roughly) of Lorenzo da Ponte (author of the libretto for *Don Giovanni*), with whom Stendhal has apparently confused him.

157

Trans.]. Certainly the Viennese oligarchy was never known to tolerate license on the stage. Well! In 1787, during the scene of the ball, Don Giovanni, Donna Anna, and Donna Elvira sang "Long live liberty!" for five minutes. At Louvois, in 1825, in an age when we are obliged to endure the speeches of General Foy and M. de Chateaubriand, Don Giovanni had to be ordered to sing "Long live hilarity!" Is it not hilarity that we lack?

In 1787, no one even thought of applauding liberty. Today there is good reason to fear that this word may become a banner. War has been declared. The privileged persons are very few in number, rich, and *envied*. Satire would be a terrible arm against them. Was it not the only enemy that Bonaparte feared? And so there must be censors, unless you want to close the theatres.

Can comedy survive this state of affairs? Will not the novel, which gets around censorship, become the successor of that poor, deceased thing? Will the courtiers, in the well-founded terror that they feel at the sound of laughter, tolerate mockery of the *class* of lawyers, the *class* of doctors, the *class* of composers who damn Rossini, the *class* of those who peddle crosses, and of the opticians who buy them? Will they tolerate the literary treatment of such an amusing subject as "The Man of Letters, or the Twenty Positions" or "The Fortune Hunter"? Are not all these *classes* of ridiculous people natural protectors who have formed a coalition for maintaining what is called *"public decency"*?

Is not the maintenance of tranquility the primary need of the police? What do they care if there is one less masterpiece? The first violation of the *unity of place* in *Christophe Colomb* resulted in the death of a man in the orchestra.

Looking at it from another angle, if we ever have complete liberty, who will give a thought to writing masterpieces? Everybody will be working, and nobody will read, except for big newspapers *in folio*, where every truth will be proclaimed in the most direct and clear terms. When this happens, French comedy will have complete freedom. But in losing Sainte-Pélagie and the Salle Saint-Martin, we shall at the same time have lost the spirit required to write, and to appreciate, comedy: that brilliant mélange of accuracy in manners and morals, light gaiety, and piquant satire. Under a monarchy, the friendship of a Louis XIV is required for a Molière to be possible. While we are waiting for such a happy stroke of fortune, and in view of the bitter criticisms directed by the Chambers and society in general against the men in power (which by no means puts them in a mood to tolerate satire), we should try romantic tragedy on the stage. At home, we should read novels and play games with *bold* proverbs.

Since the Constitutional Charter, when a young d[uke] enters a salon, he arouses feelings of malevolence in everybody there;

and he himself is embarrassed. From this I conclude that the d[ukes] will have a great deal of merit in the future, and along with it, all the *hilarity* of an English lord.

Thus the Charter: (1) takes away leisure; (2) separates by hate; (3) kills subtlety of wit. On the other hand, we are indebted to it for the eloquence of General Foy.

Letter VI

The Romantic to the Classicist

Paris, April 30, 1824

SIR,

As soon as one starts to talk about *prose tragedy on national themes* to an author who writes in verse, it provokes in him an ill-disguised abhorrence scarcely concealed behind the benignity of an academic smile. But this is by no means true of those men, full of positive ideas and an unlimited respect for good box office sales, who head the management of the theatres. On the contrary, the actors and financial directors are aware that some day (but perhaps in twelve or fifteen years: for them, this is the whole question) Romanticism will make a million for some lucky theatre in Paris.

A financial director from one of these theatres to whom I was talking about Romanticism and his future triumph, told me himself: "I understand your idea. For twenty years, *the historical novel* was derided in Paris. The Academy learnedly demonstrated the absurdity of this genre; and we all believed it. Then Sir Walter Scott appeared, holding up his *Waverley*. Balantyne, his publisher, recently died a millionaire.

"The only barrier between the box office and excellent sales," the director continued, "is the feeling at the big colleges of law and medicine, and the liberal newspapers which guide the taste of those young men. What you would have to have is a financial director rich enough to buy the literary opinion of *Le Constitutionnel* and two or three small newspapers. Until that happens, would you advise any of our theatres to present a romantic drama, in five acts and in prose, entitled *The Death of the Duc de Guise at Blois,* or *Joan of Arc and the English,* or *Clovis and the Bishops?* Can you name any theatre where such a tragedy would get as far as the third act? The editors of the influential papers (most of whom have verse plays now being performed or in rehearsal) tolerate melodrama *à la* D'Arlincourt. But they would never tolerate *melodrama written in a reasonable style.* If things were different, do you think we would not have tried Schiller's *William Tell?* The police would cut it by one-fourth; one of our adapters by another fourth; and what was left would run for a hundred performances, *provided it lasted through three.* But this is just what will never be allowed by the editors of the liberal papers—and, consequently, by the students at the colleges of law and medicine."

"But, monsieur, the great majority of young people in society were converted to Romanticism by the eloquence of M. Cousin. They all applaud the good theories of the *Globe."*

"Monsieur, your young people of good society do not come to the orchestra to get into fist fights. And in the theatre as in politics, we have only contempt for philosophers who do not get into fist fights."

I must confess that this lively and frank conversation pained me more than all the wrath of the Academy. The next day I sent inquiries to the reading rooms of the Rue Saint-Jacques and the Rue de l'Odéon. I asked for a list of the most-read books. It is no longer Racine, Molière, *Don Quixote,* etc., that the law students and medical students read to the point of wearing out three or four copies every year. Now it is Laharpe's *Cours de littérature*—so deeply is the mania for criticism rooted in the national character, so great is the need of our apprehensive vanity to bring ready-made ideas into conversation.

If M. Cousin were still giving his course, that professor's fascinating eloquence and unlimited influence on youth might perhaps bring about the conversion of the students at the big schools. Those young people would pride themselves on reciting, parrotlike, other phrases than those of Laharpe. But then M. Cousin speaks too well ever to be allowed to speak again.

As for the editors of *Le Constitutionnel* and the fashionable newspapers, it would require strong arguments to have any hope. Because they largely determine what will be successful, those gentlemen will always have the lucrative idea of themselves writing beautiful plays of the routine kind easiest to put together. Or at any rate, they will associate with the authors.

It would therefore be useful if a few modest writers who recognize that they do not have the talent necessary to create a tragedy, would devote a week or two every year to publishing a literary pamphlet in order to furnish French youth with *ready-made phrases.*

If I were fortunate enough to hit upon a few pretty phrases that would bear repetition, perhaps those very independent young people would finally understand that what one should look for at the theatre is *dramatic pleasure,* and not the epic pleasure of hearing an actor recite some very pretty and very sonorous lines *that they already know by heart,* as M. Duviquet says so naïvely.[1]

Without anyone's being aware of it, Romanticism has made great progress in the past year. People of generous minds, having despaired of politics since the last elections, have gone into literature. They have brought some good sense into it, and this is why the men of letters are so deeply chagrined.

The enemies of prose tragedy on national themes or of Romanticism (for, like M. Auger, I have discussed only the drama[2]), are of four kinds:

1) The old *classical* rhetoricians, formerly the colleagues and rivals of the Laharpes, the Geoffroys, and the Auberts.

2) The members of the Académie Française, who, owing to the splendor of their title, believe they are obliged to show themselves the worthy successors of those victims of impotent rage who criticized *Le Cid* in the old days.

3) Those authors who make money writing tragedies in verse, and those who, by means of their tragedies and despite the hissing of the audience, obtain pensions.

The most fortunate of these poets (those applauded by the public), because they are at the same time liberal journalists, determine the success of first performances; and they will never tolerate the performance of works more interesting than their own.

[1] *Le Journal des débats,* July 8, 1818.
[2] Page 7 of the *Manifesto.*

4) The least formidable of the enemies of prose tragedy on national themes, like Charles VII and the English, the *Jacques bons Hommes*,[3] Bouchard and the Monks of Saint-Denis, or Charles IX, are the *poètes associés des bonnes-lettres*. Although strongly inimical to prose in their capacity as versemakers in the manner of the Hotel de Rambouillet, and though they particularly detest a prose which is simple, correct, and unpretentious, modeled after that of Voltaire, they cannot without self-contradiction oppose the development of a kind of tragedy that will draw upon the violent passions and frightful customs of the Middle Ages for its chief effects. As loyal men of letters, presided over by M. de Chateaubriand, they would not dare to ban (for fear of vexing their noble patrons) a system of tragedy that will dwell upon the great names of the Montmorencys, the La Trimouilles, the Crillons, and the Lautrecs; and they will exhibit to the public the deeds (admittedly savage, but also great and generous, insofar as one could be those things in the twelfth century) of the warriors who founded those illustrious families.[4] After having been at a performance of a tragedy at which he saw that fierce and bloody hero, the Connétable de Montmorency, fight and die, even the most liberal voter (and the most annoyed by the sleight-of-hand tricks played upon him at the last e[lections]) will be unable to resist a kind of benevolent curiosity when he hears a Montmorency announced in a salon.

[3] Jacques Bonhomme is a conventional name for the French peasant. [Translator's note.]
[4] One can find three or four subjects for tragedy in every volume of M. Buchon's Froissart: Edward II and Mortimer; Robert d'Artois and Edward III; Jacques d'Artevelle or the Gantois; Wat Tyler; Henri de Transtamare and Du Guesclin; Jeanne de Montfort, Duchess of Brittany; Captain de Buch at Meaux; Clisson and the Duke of Brittany (the subject of *Adélaïde du Guesclin*); King John and the King of Navarre at Rouen; Gaston de Foix and his father; Gand's second rebellion under Philippe d'Artevelle. Love, that sentiment of the moderns that had not yet been born in the time of Sophocles, animates most of these subjects; for example, the love story of Limousin and Raimbaud.

Today, no one in society knows the history of France. Before M. de Barante, it was too boring to read. Romantic tragedy will teach it to us, and in a way favorable to the great men of our medieval period. This kind of tragedy, which owing to the absence of the alexandrine will inherit all the artless and sublime sayings in our old chronicles,[5] is thus completely in the interest of the Chamber of Peers. Therefore, the salon of the *Bonnes-Lettres,* which is in the retinue of that Chamber, cannot oppose with any great excess of abuse the development of prose tragedy on national themes. Moreover, once this genre is tolerated, what a fine opportunity it will provide for agreeable flattery and servile dedications! Tragedy on national themes is a great boon to the *Bonnes-Lettres.*

As for the poor Academy, which believes itself obliged to persecute, in advance, *prose tragedy on national themes,* it is a lifeless body that cannot strike any very dangerous blows. Far from killing others, the Academy will have its hands full just staying alive. Already, those of its members whom I (along with the public) respect are honored for their writings and not for the empty title of academician that they share with so many literary nullities. Even if the Académie Française were the opposite of what it is now—i.e., an assemblage of those forty persons reputed in France to have the most intelligence, genius, or talent—it could not, in this fault-finding age, attempt without risk of ridicule, to dictate to the public what literary opinions it should hold. There is no one more recalcitrant than the Parisian of today when he is ordered to believe something. (I of course make an exception of the opinion he must ostensibly hold in order to keep his position[6] or to be on the first list of those receiving the cross of the Legion of Honor.) The Academy has shown a lack of

[5] "Beaumanoir, drink your blood." (Said to Jean, Sire de Beaumanoir, by one of his knights, after the "Battle of the Thirty," against the English, in 1352. [Trans.])

[6] One of my neighbors has just cancelled his subscription to the *Journal des débats* (February, 1825) because his third son is supernumerary in a ministry.

164

tact in this whole business. It has thought of itself as a ministry. Romanticism puts it in a temper, just as Newton's philosophy or the circulation of the blood did to the Sorbonne in the past. It is easy to see why, because the positions are parallel. But was this any reason for hurling at the public, with such a comical air of superiority,[7] the opinion that it is trying to stuff into the heads of Parisians?

The Academy should have begun by taking up a collection among those honorable members whose *Complete Works* are going to be made obsolete by Romanticism: MM. de Jouy, Duval, Andrieux, Raynouard, Campenon, Levis, Baour-Lormian, Soumet,[8] Villemain, *et al.* With the goodly sum collected in this manner, it should have paid the *Débats* for the five hundred subscribers it was going to cause the latter to lose, and then published in that paper (which has been so amusing for the past two weeks) two articles every week against the romantics. My readers already have some idea, from the quotation from the *Pandore* previously given in a footnote, of the Voltairean wit and urbanity that M. de Jouy would have contributed to this debate. The columns of the *Journal des débats* would soon have been embellished with backstreet language. M. Andrieux, writing incognito, has crushed us in the *Revue.* Because the prose of the author of *Le Trésor* is as pallid as the humor in his comedies, his famous satire against the romantics would have been published in the *Débats.* If, against all appearances, this blow had not been enough to demolish them, the elegant M. Villemain,

---

[7] "Will the Académie Française remain indifferent to the alarms sounded by men of taste? . . . Shall the first literary assemblage of France be afraid of compromising itself? . . . This ceremony seemed the most favorable occasion for enunciating the principles by which the Academy is unanimously animated . . . for trying to *allay doubts, settle uncertainties,* etc." (Page 3 of the *Manifesto.*)

[8] "The God who gave us light does not forbid us to love." (*Saul, tragédie.*) The romantics propose: ". . . does not forbid us to see clearly."

overjoyed to have a bit of thought to put into his pretty phrases,[9] would not have refused the Academy the support of his rhetoric.

Instead of calling upon the wit of Voltaire's successor or the pretty verbiage of the author of *L'Histoire de Cromwell,* the Academy told us, in the dry, rasping voice of M. Auger:

> A new schism is rearing its head today. Many persons reared in a religious respect for ancient doctrines are frightened at the progress being made by this new *sect,* and seem to be asking for reassurance. . . . The danger is not yet great, and there is perhaps reason to fear that it might only be increased if we grant it too much importance. . . . But must we then wait until this *sect,* carried beyond its own goal, achieves such power that it perverts by *illegitimate* successes that floating mass of opinions always at the disposal of Fortune?[10]

Will it seem improper if an obscure person like myself looks for a moment at the successes, *legitimate* or not, of that *floating mass* which makes up the majority of this Academy? I will be careful to avoid any malicious allusion to the private lives of those authors whose glory I am attacking. Such degrading weapons are used only by the weak.

Thus those Frenchmen who decide they agree with the romantics are *sectarians.*[11] I am a *sectarian.* M. Auger, who receives extra payment for working on the *Dictionary,* cannot be unaware that this word is *odious.* If I had the urbanity of M. de Jouy, I would be entitled to use a vulgar expression in replying to the Academy. But I respect myself too much to fight the Academy with its own weapons.

What would the public, *sectarian* or not, say if asked to choose between the following on the basis of intelligence and talent?

[9] "Making pretty phases is nothing," said M. de T . . . , after hearing the young professor. "You must also have something to put into them."
[10] Pages 2 and 3 of the *Manifesto.*
[11] *"Sectarian.* This word is *odious,"* says the *Dictionnaire de l'Académie.*

M. DROZ	and M. DE LARMARTINE
M. CAMPENON, author of *l'Enfant prodigue*	and M. DE BERANGER
M. DE LACRETELLE, junior, historian	and M. DE BARANTE
M. ROGER, author of *L'Avocat*	and M. FIEVEE
M. MICHAUD	and M. GUIZOT
M. DAGUESSEAU	and M. DE LA MENNAIS
M. VILLAR	and M. VICTOR COUSIN
M. DE LEVIS	and M. le général FOY
M. DE MONTESQUIOU	and M. ROYER-COLLARD
M. DE CESSAC	and M. FAURIEL
M. le marquis DE PASTORET	and M. DAUNOU
M. AUGER, the author of thirteen book reviews	and M. PAUL-LOUIS COURIER
M. BIGOT DE PREAMENEU	
M. le comte FRAYSSINOUS, author of "A Funeral Oration for H. M. Louis XVIII"	and M. BENJAMIN CONSTANT and M. DE PRADT, former Archbishop of Malines
M. SOUMET	and M. SCRIBE
M. LAYA, author of *Falkland*	and M. ETIENNE

No line of argument could be more frank or more noble than the simple asking of this question. I am too polite to abuse my advantages. I will not repeat the answer of the public.

Because, owing to the obscurity of my life, I am not personally acquainted with any of the distinguished men figuring therein, I have all the less compunction about publishing the names in the second column, who constitute the pride of France. I am even less acquainted with the academicians whose names pale beside those of the former. Because the men in both groups exist for me only in their writings, in repeating the judgment of the public I have been able to consider myself, in a certain sense, as already representing posterity for them.

There has always been a bit of divergence between the opinion of the public and the decisions of the Academy. The public would favor the election of a talented man of whom the Academy usually was envious. For example, it nominated M. de Chateaubriand only upon express order from the Emperor. But never until now has the public gone so far as to find replacements for the majority of the Académie Française. The annoying thing is that when public opinion is defied to this extent, it retreats. The disfavor into which the Academy has fallen because of the "Luncheon" can only increase, because the majority of those men whose talent the public admires will never be chosen for membership.

The Academy became null and void the day it had the misfortune to see its members named by government order. Since receiving such a fatal blow, that assemblage, which cannot have any real existence except one based on public opinion, has been clumsy enough to miss every opportunity to recapture it. Never the least little act of courage; always the most florid and least noble servility. The good M. Montyon establishes an award for *virtue*. At this word, the ministry takes fright. M. Villemain, who is presiding over the Academy that day, wins the prize most cleverly. And the Academy, without saying a word, allows itself to be deprived of the right to confer the award. The prize is ridiculous. But it is even more ridiculous to let oneself be abased to that point—and by what kind of people! What would the ministers have done if twenty members of the Academy had resigned? But this improper idea is as far removed from the poor French Academy, as that body itself is removed from having any influence on public opinion.

I advise it to be polite in the future. Then the public, *sectarian* or not, will let it die in peace.

I remain, respectfully, etc.

The Romantic to the Classicist

Paris, May 1, 1824

SIR,

Do you mean to tell me that you believe the *Journal des débats* is an authority in literature?

Must we then disturb the repose of those old rhetoricians who are still living off the ghost of Geoffroy? Since the day when the death of that amusing person almost killed their newspaper, this assemblage of old-fashioned critics has been kept going by the *lively talent* of M. Fiévée. But its membership is dwindling. These are people who have not accepted a new idea since 1789. And the thing that discredits their literary doctrines once and for all is the fact that they are enslaved to the treasurer of the newspaper. Even if these gentlemen wanted to praise a song by Béranger or a pamphlet by Courier, the owners of the *Débats*, who are veritable Girondins of the Royalist reactionary group, would never let them do it.

That witty man who signs charming articles with the letter *A* is supposed to be one of the strongest supporters of outmoded ideas. When he writes them, one finds pleasant and stimulating things in those articles (usually so depressing) that the *Débats* publishes by way of scolding the present generation for not thinking the way people thought in 1725. Recently, when that newspaper dared to attack one of the giants of liberal literature, M. de Jouy, it was Monsieur A who was given the assignment of twitting that famous man about the great pains he takes to let us know he is very humorous and to adorn with his own portrait (as he tells us) each new literary work he gives to the public. Monsieur A even went so far as to bring more serious charges against M. de Jouy by accusing him of ignorance. He invoked the

Latin word, *agreabilis,* which I am told was not very agreeable to the author of *Sylla,* etc., etc. I don't know how well founded all these reproaches are; but here is a little example of the profound knowledge of *Messieurs les écrivains classiques.*

In the *Journal des débats* for May 22, 1823, Monsieur A attempts to review (in three enormous columns, because the classicists are weighty) some book or other in which M. le vicomte de Saint-Chamans attacks the romantics. Monsieur A says:

> In the day of *l'Homme aux quarante écus* a Scotsman, M. Home, was criticizing the most beautiful passages in Racine's *Iphigénie* just as, today, M. Schlegel criticizes the most beautiful passages in *Phèdre.* And, like the German of our day, the Scotsman of that period cited the divine Shakespeare as the true model of taste. As an example of the best style of discourse for heroes of tragedy, he quotes a speech of Lord Falstaff, the chief justice, who in the tragedy of *Henry IV,* as he is delivering to the king a prisoner he has just taken, says to him with as much wit as dignity:
>
>> "Here he is, and here I yield him: and I beseech your grace, let it be booked with the rest of this day's deeds; or . . . I will have it in a particular ballad else, with mine own picture on the top on 't . . . to the which course if I be enforced, if you do not all show like gilt twopences to me, and I in the clear sky of fame o'ershine you as much as the full moon doth the cinders of the element, which show like pins' heads to her."
>
> I thought it best to omit a few expressions, likewise far too romantic.

Is there any schoolboy today who doesn't know that Falstaff is not a great judge or a lord but a false hero full of wit —a very humorous character as famous in England as Figaro is in France? Should the classical rhetoricians be accused of

170

bad faith or of ignorance? Really, I think ignorance would be preferable.

I am afraid I would strain your patience if I gave other examples of the knowledge of these gentlemen with respect to anything not connected with classical literature. One of them, M. Villemain, who according to his own newspaper refutes the errors of the romantics—*and from such a lofty position of authority*[1]—goes so far as to locate the Orinoco River in North America.[2]

Please accept, etc.

[1] The *Journal des débats*, March, 1823.
[2] Book IV of *Les Théâtres étrangers*, p. 325.

Letter VIII

The Romantic to the Classicist

Andilly, May 3, 1824

SIR,

You tell me that I only find reasons for destroying things; that I never rise above the a facile talent for pointing out shortcomings. You grant me that the liberal papers are forming the opinions of youth. Also, that the *Journal des débats*, while judging Shakespeare and Schiller without having read them, is misleading the older generation, who, like the young people, do not like to read new masterpieces that require the effort of thinking, but prefer ready-made phrases. The dramatic genre, which has done more than all others to make France illustrious, has been sterile for many years. In London and Naples the only things they are translating are the charming plays of M. Scribe or melodramas. What is to be done?

1) Entrust the duties of censorship to gentle and reasonable men who will give free rein to M. Lermercier, M. Andrieux, and other sensible persons who are the enemies of scandal.

2) Dethrone the glory of theatrical premieres. In Italy, premieres are of hardly any importance. Every new opera, however bad, is performed three times. It is the right of the maestro, they say. Rossini's *Barber of Seville* was not completed at Rome the first night and did not triumph until the night following.

Would it not be reasonable to require our theatres to perform new plays three times? Could not the all-powerful police absolutely rule out free tickets from these first three performances?

If they were sensible, those of the public who were bored the first night would not come back the second night. But good Lord! How far we are from being this tolerant in matters of literature! Our young people, who are so liberal when they are talking about constitutions, juries, elections, etc.—in short, about power that they do not possess, and how they would use it—become as ridiculously despotic as any little cabinet minister when they themselves have some power to exercise. In the theatre, they have the power of hissing. Well! Not only do they hiss things that seem bad to them (which is perfectly right) but they will not let other spectators, who are entertained by what they themselves think is bad, enjoy their pleasure.

For example, the young liberals, excited by the *Constitutionnel* and the *Miroir,* drove the English actors off the stage of the theatre at the Porte Saint-Martin and deprived of a very lively pleasure those Frenchmen who, rightly or wrongly, like this kind of play. It is well known that the hissing and booing began before the curtain was raised on the English play, of which not a word could be heard. As soon as the actors appeared they were pelted with apples and eggs. Every now and then someone would shout at them: "Speak French!" In a word, it was a fine triumph for the *national honor!*

The sensible people said to one another: "Why did they come to the play if they didn't know the language?" They were told that most of the young people had been persuaded of the strangest kind of stupidities. Some young shop clerks even went so far as to shout: *"Down with Shakespeare! He's an aide-de-camp of the Duke of Wellington!"*

What a miserable business! What a shameful thing for the leaders as well as the led! I can see no difference between our students, who are so liberal, and the censors, who are the objects of their scorn. These two groups are equally liberal; and they have the same respect for justice when they ban plays which do not suit them. They use the same kind of arguments: *force.* And we know what feelings force arouses in human hearts when it is separated from justice.

Instead of trying to judge things on the basis of *Literary principles* and defending *sound doctrines,*[1] why don't our young people content themselves with the finest privilege of

[1] M. Duviquet, in the *Débats* for November 12, 1824.

173

their age: that of having feelings? If young Frenchmen of twenty, living in Paris and trained in reasoning by the lessons of the Cuviers and the Daunous, were able to consult their own particular way of feeling and to judge only from their own hearts, no audience in Europe would be comparable to that of the Odéon. But in that case perhaps no one would applaud lines like

The age of his forefathers borders on the cradle of the world.
Le Paria

A librarian I know, who makes a show of classical opinions (because otherwise he might very well lose his job) has just given me, secretly, a list of the books most frequently called for at his library. There, just as in the reading rooms of the Rue de l'Odéon, Laharpe is read much more than Racine and Molière.

Laharpe's great fame came after his death. Although while he lived he was a rather insignificant pedant (because he had no Greek and little Latin, and in French literature he had no suspicion of what had preceded Boileau), he has since become a Father of the classical church. Here is why.

When Napoleon suspended the Revolution (believing, like us, that it was over), there was an entire generation that had no literary education whatsoever. This generation knew, however, that an old literature existed; and it was looking forward to enjoying the plays of Racine and Voltaire. With the restoration of order, everyone's first thought was of acquiring status. There was a fever of ambition. None of us had the idea that a new literature could be born out of that same new order into which we were entering. We were French; that is to say, not lacking in vanity, and most eager, not to read Homer, but to judge Homer. Leharpe's *Cours de littérature,* famous from 1787 on, was ready and waiting to supply our needs. Hence its immense success.

How can we make our law students forget this code of literature? Wait until it is worn out? But in that case thirty years would be lost. I see only one solution: the code must be revised. We must present to the avid vanity of our young people, sixteen volumes of ready-made judgments on all the literary questions one is likely to encounter in the salons.

But, you will say to me, if you preach a sound, clear, philosophical doctrine you will make people forget Laharpe's phrases.

Not at all. Literature, that poor thing, has the misfortune of being something fashionable: people for whom it is not intended insist absolutely upon talking about it.

At this point, sir, I am strongly tempted to add twenty pages by way of expansion. I would like to overwhelm the intolerant ones, both classicists and romantics, set forth the main ideas in accordance with which, in my new *Course of Literature* in sixteen volumes I will judge the dead and the living, etc.[2] But have no fear. What with the lively interest

[2] First: Never any battles or executions on the stage. These things belong to the epic, not the drama. In the nineteenth century the heart of the spectator is repulsed by the horrible; and when, in Shakespeare, the hangman comes forward to burn out the eyes of little children, instead of shuddering the audience laughs at the broom handles with the ends painted red to resemble bars of iron heated red-hot.

Second: The more romantic the ideas and incidents (i.e., the more they are based on present-day needs), the more one must respect language—*which is a thing agreed upon*—in turns of phrase no less than in words, and try to write like Pascal, Voltaire, and La Bruyère. The *necessities* and *requirements* of *Messieurs les doctrinaires* will be as ridiculous in fifty years as Voiture and Balzac [i.e., Guez de Balzac. Trans.] are today. Cf. the Preface to *L'Histoire des ducs de Bourgogne*.

Third: The rapt attention with which one follows the emotions of a character constitutes *tragedy;* that mere curiosity which leaves all our attention free for a hundred different details constitutes *comedy*. The feeling aroused in us by *Julie d'Etanges* is tragic. Shakespeare's *Coriolanus* is comedy. The mixing of these two kinds of interest strikes me as very difficult.

Fourth: Unless it is necessary to portray the successive changes wrought in the character of a man by the passage of time, perhaps it will be felt that a tragedy should not cover several years, if it is to please audiences in 1825. In any case, each playwright will do his own experimenting, as a result of which it may turn out that one year will be found a suitable length of time. If the tragedy were to be prolonged much beyond that, the hero of its ending would not be the same man as in the beginning. Napoleon wrapped up in the imperial mantle in 1804 was no longer the

of our political situation, I maintain that any pamphlet of more than a hundred pages, or any work of more than two volumes, will never be read.

Then, too, the romantics are not concealing the fact that

---

young general of 1796, who hid his glory under that gray overcoat which will be his costume for posterity.

Fifth: It is his *art* that one must borrow from Shakespeare, while yet realizing that this young workman in woolen clothing earned fifty thousand francs of income by exerting his influence on the English of the year 1600, who were already beginning to be aroused by all the gloomy and dull horrors they found in the Bible, out of which they created Puritanism. A natural and somewhat stupid (Cf. the diatribe of M. Martin against the experiments of our renowned Magendie in the House of Commons, session of February 24, 1825.) sincerity, complete dedication, a kind of difficulty in understanding little incidents and being moved by them, but on the other hand a great constancy of emotion and a great fear of Hell—these things separate the Englishman of 1600 from the Frenchman of 1825. But it is the latter we must please —those people who are so subtle, so impressionable, always on the watch, always a prey to a fleeting emotion, and always incapable of deep feeling. They believe in nothing but the latest vogue, but they simulate all convictions—not out of a calculating hypocrisy like the *cant* of the English upper classes, but simply in order to play their role well in the eyes of others.

Major Bridgenorth, in *Peveril of the Peak,* whose father had seen Shakespeare, behaves with a morose and gloomy sincerity in accordance with absurd principles. Our ethics are almost perfect; but on the other hand there is no more boundless dedication to be found, except for the speeches published in the *Moniteur.* The Parisian respects only the opinion of those he sees every day. He is dedicated only to his mahogany furniture. Thus in order to write romantic dramas (adapted to the needs of the age), it will be necessary to diverge widely from Shakespeare's manner and, for example, not get bogged down in tirades for a public that understands everything beautifuly and at the slightest hint, whereas for the English of the year 1600 it was necessary to explain things at length, using many strong images.

Sixth: After having learned the *art* from Shakespeare, we must turn to Gregory of Tours, Froissart, Livy, the Bible, and the modern Hellenes for subjects of tragedy. What story is more beautiful and more moving than the death of Jesus? Why were the manuscripts of Sophocles and Homer discovered only in 1600, after the civilization of the age of Leo X?

Madame du Hausset, Saint-Simon, Gourville, Dangeau, Bézen-

they are proposing to the Parisians the most difficult thing in the world: a change of habits. A vain person, once he has dared to give up a habit, is exposed to the frightful risk of being nonplussed in the face of an objection. Is there any-

---

val, the diplomatic congresses, the Phanar of Constantinople, and the stories of the conclaves gathered by Gregorio Leti will provide us with a hundred subjects for comedy.

Seventh: We have been told: *Poetry is the ideal beauty of expression.* Given an idea, poetry is the *most beautiful* way to express it—the manner in which it will have the greatest effect.

Yes, for a satire, an epigram, a satirical comedy, an epic poem, or mythological tragedy like *Phèdre, Iphigénie,* etc.

No, when it is a question of that kind of tragedy which gets its effects from the exact portrayal of the emotions and the incidents in the lives of contemporaries. In the dramatic genre, the thought or feeling must *above all* be expressed clearly—in which respect it is the opposite of the epic genre. *"The table is full,"* cries Macbeth, trembling with terror when he sees the ghost of Banquo, whom he had had murdered an hour before, sitting down at the royal table in the place reserved for him, King Macbeth. What verse, what rhythm, could add to the beauty of such an exclamation?

It is a cry of the heart; and a cry of the heart does not allow of inversion. Is it as part of an alexandrine that we admire lines like, *"Let us be friends, Cinna,"* or Hermione's question to Pyrrhus: *"Who told you?"*

Note that it is exactly those words, and no others, that are needed. When the cadence of the verse does not allow using the exact word that an impassioned man would say, what do our poets of the Academy do? They betray the feeling for the alexandrine. Very few persons, especially at eighteen, know the passions well enough to exclaim: "This is the required word that you are leaving out. The one you are using is only a cold synonym." Whereas the most stupid person in the orchestra knows very well what makes a pretty verse. And he knows even better (because under a monarchy, all of a person's vanity depends upon it) what word belongs to *noble diction* and what does not.

In this respect the refinements of French drama have gone well beyond those of nature. A king coming at night to an enemy house asks his confidant: "What time is it?" Well, the author of *Le Cid d'Andalousie* did not dare to have the man reply: "Sire, it is midnight." That man of wit had the courage to write two lines of poetry:

La tour de Saint-Marcos, près de cette demeure,
A, comme vous passiez, sonné la douzieme heure.

177

thing surprising in the fact that of all the peoples in the world, the French are the most tenacious of their habits? It is the dread of obscure perils—perils that compel one to *invent* unusual and perhaps *ridiculous* courses of action—that makes *moral* courage so rare.

(The tower of Saint-Marcos, which is near this dwelling, struck twelve o'clock as you were passing.)

I will develop elsewhere the theory of which the following is a mere outline. It is the function of poetry to concentrate in one place—by means of ellipses, inversions, groupings of words, etc., etc. (the brilliant privileges of poetry)—the reasons for apprehending a beauty of nature. Now in the dramatic genre it is the *preceding scenes* that provide all the effect of the word we hear said in the immediate scene. For example: *"Do you know the handwriting of Rutilius?"* (Lord Byron approved this distinction.)

If the character tries by means of poetic expression to add to the force of what he is saying, he falls to the level of a mere speechmaker *whom I mistrust,* however little experience of life I may have.

The first requirement of drama is that the action take place in a room one of whose walls has been removed by the magic wand of Melpomene and replaced by the orchestra. The characters do not know that there is an audience. Is there any trusted retainer of a king who, in a moment of peril, would take it into his head not to answer briefly and to the point when the king asks him: *"What time is it?"* The moment there is an obvious concession to the audience, there are no more dramatis personae. I see only rhapsodists reciting a more or less beautiful epic poem. In French, the dominion of rhythm or of poetry begins only when *inversion is permitted.*

This note would grow into a volume, if I attempted to challenge all the absurdities that the poor poetasters, fearing for their prestige in society, preach every morning to the romantics. The classicists are in possession of the theatres and all the literary positions for which the government pays salaries. Young men are put in vacant positions only when sponsored by older men *working in the same faction.* Fanaticism is one of the qualifications for a job. All the servile ones—all those with petty aspirations toward professorships, the academies, library positions, etc.—*have an interest* in giving us, every morning, articles in support of classicism. And, unfortunately, declamation in all the genres is the eloquence of that indifference which pretends to be a burning faith.

At any rate, it is rather amusing that at a time when the literary reform is represented by all the newspapers as having been put

Finally, sir, I must ask your indulgence for the length of my letters and especially for the rather drab simplicity of my style. I have passed over, for purposes of clarity, many new ideas that would have been most pleasing to my vanity. I wanted not only to be lucid, but to leave no opportunity for persons of bad faith to exclaim: "Good Heavens! How obscure these romantics are in their explanations!"

I am, respectfully, etc.

---

down, they are still obliged to hurl at it, every morning, some new stupidity which, like *Lord Falstaff, a great English judge,* gives us something to laugh at for the rest of the day. Does it not seem that this kind of behavior has the look of a defeat in the making?

Letter IX

The Classicist to the Romantic

Paris, May 3, 1824

SIR,

You might be interested to know that, if memory serves me right, it has been many long years since I have written four letters on the same subject in one day.

I confess that I am moved by your deep respect for Racine —deeply moved. I had had the impression that, not yourself, but the romantic faction was unjust and—if I may venture to say so—insolent toward that great man. I seemed to see that faction

> Burlesquement roidir ses petits bras
> Pour étouffer si haute renommée.

(Ludicrously tighten the muscles in his little arms so as to choke such great renown.)

Lebrun

I found it amusing that several men of intelligence had imagined they could give the public a theory (because you will admit that your Romanticism is only a theory) by means of which one is sure to get masterpieces. I note with pleasure that you do not believe that any dramatic system can create minds like those of Molière or Racine. Although I certainly do not approve your theory, sir, I do believe I understand it. There remain, however, many obscure points and many questions I must ask you. For example, what in your opinion is the farthest point of the success of the romantic genre? Must I absolutely accustom myself to these heroes rejected in advance by the legislator of Parnassus, who are

Children in the first act, and graybeards in the last?[1]

[1] From Chant III of Boileau's *Art Poétique: Là, souvent, le héros d'un spectacle grossier/Enfant au premier acte, est barbon au dernier.* [Translator's note.]

Let us suppose for a moment that the good traditions die out and that good taste disappears—in a word, that everything turns out just as you want it—and that the great actor who follows in the footsteps of Talma is willing, twenty years from now, to perform in your prose tragedy entitled *The Death of Henri III*. What, in your opinion, will be the farthest point reached in this revolution? Set aside all Jesuitical prudence in answering me, and be frank in what you say, like the Hostpur [sic] of your Shakespeare—with whom, by the way, I am very well satisfied.

I am, etc.

Letter X

The Romantic to the Classicist

Andilly, May 5, 1824

SIR,

If we return to this world about the year 1864, we shall find on the streetcorners, posters advertising:

THE RETURN FROM ELBA
A prose tragedy in five acts

By this time, the colossal figure of Napoleon will have made people forget the Caesars, the Fredericks, etc., for a few centuries. The first act of the tragedy, which will present to the French public the most astonishing action in history, must obviously take place on the island of Elba, the day of the embarkation. Napoleon is on stage, impatient of rest and thinking of France. "Upon my return from Egypt, across this same sea, which encircles my country, Fortune smiled at me. Is it possible she has abandoned me?" At this point he pauses to observe with his long-glass a frigate flying a white flag which is disappearing into the distance.

A military police officer in disguise makes his appearance, bringing the most recent issues of the *Quotidienne*. A courier who has come from Vienna in six days tells him he is to be transferred to St. Helena, and collapses at his feet from fatigue.

Napoleon makes his decision: he gives orders for the departure. The audience sees the grenadiers embarking and hears them singing on the brig *l'Actif*. An inhabitant of Elba displays amazement. An English spy, instead of giving his signal, becomes completely drunk and collapses under the table. An assassin, who had come disguised as a priest, swears and curses at God because he has failed to earn the million promised to him.

The second act should take place near Grenoble, at Lafrey, on the shore of the lake, and show the subornation of the First Battalion, Seventh Light Infantry, sent by General Marchant to block the narrow road between the mountain and the lake.

The third act takes place at Lyons. Napoleon has already forgotten his reasonable and popular ideas and has begun to create nobles again. The danger past, he is once more growing drunk on the pleasures of despotism.

In the fourth act we see him on the Champ de Mars with his brothers in uniforms of white satin, and his new Constitution.

The fifth act takes place at Waterloo, except for the last scene, which shows his arrival at the rock of St. Helena with the prophetic *vision* of six years of torment, petty vexations, and assassinations by pin-prick executed by Sir Hudson Lowe. There is a fine contrast between the young Dumoulin, who at Grenoble, in the first act [sic], swears fealty to Napoleon, and the impassive general who, at St. Helena, in the hope of winning a cordon of the second class, tries to kill him by inches but in such a way that his master cannot be accused of poisoning him.

Another contrast between secondary characters: M. Benjamin Constant at the Tuileries pleading the cause of a reasonable Constitution with Napoleon, who behaves in an openly despotic manner, treats France as his private domain, and talks of his, Bonaparte's, *own interests;* and, three months later, M. le comte de Las-Cases deploring, in the bitterness and sincerity of his chamberlain's heart, the fact that the Emperor had almost found himself in a situation where he had to open a door *himself.*

There, as is plain to see, you have a fine tragedy. The only things lacking are an interval of fifty years' time and the genius to write it. It is fine because it is a single event. Who could deny that?

A nation lacking the resolve to attempt . . . better[1]

---

[1] Or perhaps "prefers" (*aime mieux*); i.e., ". . . to attempt [great deeds on its own], prefers [to appeal to] a great man. . . . ," etc. [Translator's note.]

. . . a great man by his. . . . The great man has the courage to take a chance, and he succeeds. But, carried away by his love of false glory and satin uniforms, he betrays that nation and falls. A hangman takes charge of him. There you have a lofty lesson: the nation has its faults; the great man has his own faults, too.

I maintain that such a spectacle is moving; that such a dramatic pleasure is possible; that it goes better on the stage than in an epic; that a spectator who has not been stupefied by the study of Laharpe and his like, will not give the slightest thought to pretending he was shocked by the seven months of time and the five thousand leagues of space that it requires.

I am, respectfully, etc.

1816

LORD BYRON IN ITALY

An Eyewitness Account

Published in *La Revue de Paris,* March, 1830.
A note by Colomb states that 1816 is the year to which the memoir refers, 1830 being the year of actual composition.

WAS BYRON'S CONSCIENCE TROUBLED by a murder like that committed by Othello? Today, this question can harm only the one who asks it. How could it damage that great man who, for six years now, has been in his grave, whence he still strikes fear into all those hypocrites who reign supreme in haughty England?

I had a moment of compunction before I raised this question. What could be more cruel than to give the impression of paying court to the despicable and abominable hypocrisy (cant) which calls Lord Byron the leader of the Satanic school, or attacks him more adroitly by pretending to pity him for his grave mistakes?

This very deep hatred is a political hatred. Anyone who takes the trouble to read M. de Custine's account of his trip,[1] or who goes there himself, will soon become convinced that it [England] is a country governed for the exclusive benefit and glory of a thousand or twelve hundred families. The younger brothers of the lords, and their tutors, find opulence and rich livings in the church establishment. In return, they are responsible for stupefying a nation of workingmen and teaching them to respect and almost to love the aristocrats, who share all the dinners and a good third of the revenue from the taxes which crush the former. A few years ago someone was bold enough to publish a curious list of the number of pounds sterling that the family of each lord, and the lord himself, draws from the public revenue under one pretext or another: salaries, pensions, livings, sinecures, etc., etc. This list shows Lord Byron's mother and his family as receiving seventeen hundred pounds sterling.[2] Needless to say, the author and the publisher were both declared to be liars and scoundrels.

[1] A reference to De Custine's travels in Scotland. [Translator's note.]

[2] Lord Grey and his family: 5,500 pounds sterling. Page 13, 4th edition. Lord Bute and his family: 64,894 pounds sterling. Page 6. Lord Westmoreland and his family: 50,650 pounds sterling. Page 24. Lord Waterford and his family: 53,265 pounds sterling. Page 23.

I must do justice to the complete amiability and private virtues of several members of the English aristocracy. It pains me to have to attack the political position of men who are so pleasant to know. But this same aristocracy loathes Lord Byron; and it is my duty to show that its opinions can lay claim neither to disinterestedness nor to impartiality. In the English system, everything hangs together: while the church teaches the people to venerate the aristocracy, the aristocrats in turn protect the interests of the church. In private, a rich man will tell you that he has exactly the same opinions as Hume on the verities of the church. A quarter-hour later, if there are ten persons gathered around him, he will castigate with the most contemptuous names those scoundrels who dare to have doubts about the miracles or the divine mission of Jesus Christ. Now that the army has become fashionable and trade ridiculous, hypocrisy has made such rapid progress that every day one hears of the conversion of yet another philosopher who in his youth dared to make fun of the selfishness, gluttony, and infinite servility of the English priests.

The intimate union of the peers and the priests has engendered a tyranny that is both savage and cruel, because it fears what in London is called *public opinion*. This view of life adopted by the English upper classes tyrannizes England more than M. Metternich's soldiers are tyrannizing Italy. All in all, I would say that there is more freedom in Italy. Of the thirty or forty little acts that yesterday made up your day or mine, two or three, in Italy, would have been rendered impossible by the Austrian police spies. In England, every single one would have been hindered. What a sad and incredible thing! In that country, which was once so unusual, there are no more eccentrics.

Because the opinions of the English upper classes are derived from their material interests, they cannot be corrected by reason.

How strange is the fate of human things! Is it true, then, that liberty, the primary need of man, is impossible on this earth? In those countries groaning under the police of the petty despotisms of Turin, Modena, or Cassel, men yearn for the freedom of New York. And in New York, a man is less free to do what he wants than in Venice or Rome. The press, liberated from prior censorship, provides political freedom. But in order to please a prudish public, it publishes today all our little acts of yesterday. It removes all freedom from the hundred little acts which, for better or for worse, fill everyone's day. Could it actually be true that the Paris of 1830 is the freest city in the world?

Public opinion among the English upper classes ("high life"), which for a long time had been irritated by Lord Byron's outspoken manner, exploded against him a year after his marriage, when his wife left him. He was reduced to a state of despair; for although he talked philosophy like Cicero, he was by no means a philosopher. And this is all to the good, because otherwise he would not have been a great poet. The sole object of his attention was Lord Byron himself. As a result of this bad habit (the leprosy of civilization) he exaggerated his own misfortunes, as did that Jean-Jacques Rousseau with whom it angered him to be compared.

Made deeply unhappy by the deluge of caricatures, satires, pamphlets, and abuse of all kinds—which with respect to him were the executors of the terrible judgment pronounced upon him by the upper classes of his own country—Byron consoled himself with one thought: he hoped to be justified after his death. He wrote his memoirs and entrusted them to a friend. The friend threw them into the fire. To please whom? And what was the price paid?

After such a deed (no example of which, fortunately, is offered by that *immoral* country of France), the friend *dared* to reproach Byron with certain youthful follies. The poet had exaggerated them, because like the regent Duke of Orleans he loved to boast of the few vices that nature (or rather, his Cambridge education) had given him.

In 1817, Monsignore Ludovic de Brême [Ludovico di Breme], formerly first chaplain to Napoleon, the King of Italy, brought together some twelve or fifteen young men in his box at La Scala, in Milan. In accordance with an Italian custom too little followed in France, these friends would meet every evening. How can one possibly be affected toward a person one sees three hundred times a year? *Affectation*, that great *refrigerating* factor in the French salons, is completely ruled out by the arrangements of Milanese society.

Today, in 1830, almost all of M. de Brême's friends are either dead or condemned to death—although I can assure the reader that I never met men more honest than they were, or less given to conspiracy.

One evening at La Scala a rather short young man with superb eyes entered our box. As he moved toward that side of the loge overlooking the orchestra, we noticed that he limped slightly. M. de Brême said, "Gentlemen, this is Lord Byron." Then he introduced each of us to his lordship. He did this with all the ceremony that might have been managed by his grandfather, who was ambassador from the Duke of Savoy to Louis XIV.

Since we already had some experience of the English character, which flees attempts at probing it, we were careful not to speak to Lord Byron, or even to glance at him.

Among those in the box was a very handsome man with a military bearing. [With him,] Lord Byron seemed to lose some of his English chilliness.

Subsequently, we thought we surmised that Lord Byron was at once enthusiastic about Napoleon and envious of him. He would say, "He and I are the only ones who sign our names N.B. (Noël Byron)." During the day preceding the evening when Byron came to M. de Brême's box, he had been told that he would meet someone who had taken part in the Moscow campaign. (In 1816, this event possessed the character of novelty. Those novels which have since spoiled it for us had not yet appeared.) And he took our mustachioed friend to be the one who had fled from Moscow.

The next day he became aware of his mistake and did me the honor of talking to me about Russia. I worshiped Napoleon; and I replied to Byron as to a member of that legislative chamber that had recently handed the great man over to the hangman of St. Helena. (For purposes of clarity in this account, the author is obliged to put himself on stage in this scene. But most assuredly it is an act of modesty rather than of pride to call attention to oneself on the same page on which Lord Byron has just been mentioned.) I had spent the previous night reading *The Corsair;* but I had none-theless promised myself that I would not depart from the coldness due a colleague of Lord Bathhurst.

The fact that I kept this vow to remain glacial explains why, a few days later, Lord Byron showed me so much kind-ness. One evening, however, in no particular connection, he said something to me about the immorality of the French character. I answered him firmly, mentioning the prison ships in which French prisoners of war are tortured, the deaths of the Russian emperors, which always happen just at the right time for England's interests, the infernal machine, etc. After this discussion, which was very polite and even respectful on my part—but basically very harsh—the others in the loge thought that Byron would never speak to me again. But the next day he took me by the arm, and we walked for an hour through the immense, empty foyers of La Scala. I was charmed by this kindness, and I deceived myself. Lord Byron had a hundred questions he wanted to put to an eyewitness of the Russian campaign. He wanted to get at the truth by trying to embarrass me. Actually, I was undergoing a cross-examination. But I did not realize it. The next night I was ecstatic as I reread *Childe Harold.* I loved Lord Byron.

He had achieved no success whatsoever among the twelve or fifteen Italians who met together every evening in Mon-signore de Brême's loge. I must confess that one evening, in the course of some argument, he gave us to understand that he should win the argument because he was a peer and a nobleman. This impertinence was by no means found accept-able. Monsignore de Brême recalled the well-known anecdote about General de Castries who, shocked by the attention being paid to d'Alembert, exclaimed: "The fellow is trying to reason, and he doesn't even have a thousand *écus* a year!"

My Italian friends found Lord Byron haughty, bizarre, and even a bit mad.

He was especially ridiculous one evening when he angrily protested that he in no way resembled Jean-Jacques Rousseau, with whom a newspaper had recently compared him. His chief reason—which he was careful not to bring out and which put him in a rage—was that Rousseau had been a servant. Moreover, he was a watchmaker's son. After the discussion, we had a hearty laugh when he asked M. de Brême, who belonged to the ranking nobility of Turin, for details on the Govon family, with whom Rousseau had been a servant. (See *Les Confessions*.)

Byron had a soul very much like that of Rousseau in the sense that *he was constantly concerned with himself and the effect he produced on others*. He is the *least dramatic* poet that ever existed. He was unable to transform himself into another person. Hence his marked hatred for Shakespeare. I believe, moreover, that he despised him because he had been able to transform himself into Shylock, a vile Jew of Venice, or Jake Cade, a miserable demagogue.

One thing that *terrified* Lord Byron was gaining weight. It was his *idée fixe*.

M. Polidori, a young doctor who was traveling with him, told us that Byron's mother was short and very dumpy. In the course of dissecting the character of Lord Byron (I must admit this was what occupied us after he had left us; and I admired the subtlety of the Italians: they are never taken in by appearances) and examining under the microscope the character of the great poet who had fallen among us like a bomb, the friends of M. de Brême decided that during one-third of the day Lord Byron was a dandy: he did not want to grow fat; [he tried] to hide his right foot (which was slightly turned in) and to charm the ladies. But in this respect, his vanity was so excessive and morbid that he forgot the end for the means. If love had interfered with his horseback riding, he would have sacrificed love. In Milan—and especially in Venice a few months later—his handsome eyes, his fine horses, and his fame aroused the beginnings of passion in several very young, very aristocratic, and certainly very beautiful women. One of them traveled more than a hundred miles to attend a masked ball at which he was to be present. He was apprised of it; but whether out of pride or timidity, he did not deign to reply to her. "He is a boor!" she exclaimed, as she moved away from him.

A failure with a woman of society would have made Byron die of wounded vanity. As a result of all those pettinesses of

English civilization, the only women he paid attention to were those who consider a lover's wealth his greatest merit.

Not content with being the most handsome man in England, Byron would also have liked to be the one most in fashion. When he was being a dandy, he would quiver with adoration and envy as he uttered the name of Brummel. (The latter was the king of fashion from 1796 to 1810. His was the most curious existence that the eighteenth century produced in England, and perhaps in Europe. This king ended his days in Calais.)

When Byron was not thinking of his handsome looks, he was thinking of his noble birth. Once, in his presence and with a very amusing show of good-hearted humor, the young men of Milan were discussing whether Henri IV could rightfully expect to be called *clement* after he had ordered the beheading of his former comrade, the Duc de Biron. "Napoleon would not have done it," Byron replied. The comical thing was that at times, as we could see, he considered himself more noble than the Duc de Biron, and then a moment later he would be envious of the eminence of that family. The fact is that very few families in England have produced a longer line of brave warriors than the Birons.

When the fatuity of good birth or handsome appearance offered him no advantages, Byron would suddenly become a great poet and a *man of sense*. He never spoke with affectation—like Mme de Staël, for example, whom he had just left at Copet, and who soon afterward came to Milan. When literature was being discussed, Byron was the opposite of an academician: always more ideas than words, and never any straining after elegance. Especially toward midnight, on these evenings when the music at the opera had moved him, instead of thinking of the effect to be produced on others as he talked, he would be carried away by his own feelings like a man of southern France.

It is a strange thing that in his prose he is always striving after wit—and wit of the most miserable kind, based on *allusion* to a passage in some classical author. I can assure the reader that nothing in the world was farther removed from his tedious prose (worthy of Archdeacon Triblet) than his charming conversation when he was not being fatuous or insane. Because it must be admitted—and for that great man it is more of an excuse than an accusation—that during one-third of the time, every week, he struck us as insane. Some people maintained that he seemed to have been driven mad by *remorse*. Was it possible, we asked ourselves, that in a fit of aristocratic or dandyish pride he had blown out the brains of a beautiful Greek slave girl who had been unfaithful to his bed?

Until such time as Parliamentary reform or some other accident has overthrown the tyranny exercised by London high society over the views of ninety-five per cent of the English with the magic word *improper*, I shall not be at all surprised to see the English reviews declare the satanic Lord Byron capable of murder. Please remember that these poor reviews cannot survive and prosper unless they are bought by the upper classes. And no one on the continent can imagine how much more aristocratic are the great English families than our most celebrated ultraroyalists. An English duke, for example, can never be ridiculous, whatever he does. (This is indeed tempting!) An academic poet named Southey has enjoyed the patronage of the upper classes because of the abuse he heaped upon Lord Byron. Once such insult was so atrocious that the great man, then at Pisa, was on the point of taking a post-carriage and returning to England to shoot Southey with his pistol. "Be careful," a friend told him. "The aristocracy will pay out money to all the bad poets, by buying their works, merely in return for the assurance that the tranquility of the author of *Don Juan* will be disturbed."

In my opinion the English aristocrats would be making a shrewd deal if they could have *Don Juan* destroyed at a cost of ten million francs. In their insane fury they even opposed the Lord Chancellor's authorization of a lawsuit by the bookseller who printed *Don Juan* against the publishers of pirated editions. As a result, England was flooded with editions of *Don Juan* selling at two shillings (two francs, fifty centimes) instead of fifteen or twenty francs. This divine poem is a cruel antagonist to the theology of Paley.

Is it not amusing to witness an anger that in its excessive

fury and blindness works against itself? I see no reason why polite society should not proclaim Byron a murderer. The bill of indictment may be found in Byron's memoirs, which Mr. Moore has just sold to the bookseller, Murray, for one hundred and fifty thousand francs.

In his journal, Byron alludes to an event the memory of which disturbs his sleep and causes him horrible agitation. He writes:

> I composed *The Bride of Abydos* in four nights, in order to drive off my dreams of ****. If I had not forced myself to this task, I should have gone mad with grief.[3]

And further on:

> I awoke from a dream. Well! Have not others dreamed? And what a dream! But she was not able to reach me. Is it true, then, that the dead cannot rest in peace? Oh, how my blood was chilled. And I could not wake up! And . . .
> ... shadows tonight
> Have struck more terror to the soul of Richard
> Than can the substance of ten thousand [soldiers]
> Armed in proof and led by shallow [Richmond].[4]

> I do not like this dream! I detest its "foregone conclusion." And am I to be taken by shadows? Ay, when they remind us of—no matter—but if I dream thus again, I will try whether *all* sleep has the like visions.

He adds:

> He [Hobhouse, mentioned above] told me an odd report that I am the actual Conrad, the veritable Corsair, and that part of my travels are supposed to have passed in privacy. Um! people sometimes hit near the truth; but never the whole truth. He don't know what I was about the year he left the Levant, nor does anyone—nor—nor—nor—however, it is a lie—but "I doubt the equivocator, the fiend that lies like truth!"

[3] Here, as elsewhere, Stendhal seems to be quoting from memory —and inaccurately. [Translator's note.]
[4] A quotation from Shakespeare's *Richard III*.

Mr. Moore does not offer any light on the foregoing. This man of wit probably did not realize that those few lines were going to provide a text for the sermons of all the priests in England and America.

But what does it matter to Lord Byron? High society can stifle a great man; but once known, he has an open account with posterity. Greece is about to become a civilized country. At Athens in 1811, in the Franciscan monastery, he had moments of insanity. This is plain from what he said to one of the monks. If there is anything real in this idea, hundreds of witnesses could be found, if necessary; and sooner or later posterity will know whether Byron's remorse was real, *or just one more affectation.*

Is Othello a man to be despised because he once gave in to the atrocious pain of jealousy?

After all, Lord Byron had a soul so easily excitable (when he was not playing the dandy) that he exaggerated his remorse over some fault committed in his youth. It was the opinion of the twelve jurymen whom fate had brought together in the loge of M. de Brême that the fault which sometimes made Byron's handsome eyes seem wild and haggard had been committed against a woman. One evening, for example, we were discussing a pretty woman of Milan who had tried to fight a duel with her lover, who had left her. Then we talked of a prince who had killed, out of hand, a lower-class woman with whom he had been living and whom he had found unfaithful. Lord Byron did not once open his mouth. He tried for a short time to contain himself, then left the box in a rage. If this was fury, it was fury against himself, and no doubt it absolves him in our eyes. I compare this crime, whatever it was, to Rousseau's theft of a ribbon when he was at Turin. Among persons who have some experience of life and are not limited to salon phrases, is there anyone who, because of what Rousseau did, would declare him less estimable than the great majority of men? It is true that toward 1815 a certain modern writer, acting on his own authority, changed the stolen ribbon into a set of silver service. And no doubt this discovery, so important to the good cause, has not gone unrewarded. It is an example of just how far we can trust vulgar historians as long as we have with us that powerful party whose hatreds are vented in persecuting the Emperor Julian, Jean-Jacques Rousseau, Lord Byron, and in fact everyone who apparently had some success in mocking at hypocrisy.

After only a few weeks, Lord Byron seemed to take very much to social life in Milan—the only society which, in the nineteenth century, allows of good-hearted humor. Often, after the opera, we would stop in the foyer to watch the pretty women pass by. Few cities have had a cluster of beautiful women who could compare to those whom chance had brought together in Milan in 1817. Several of them expected that Lord Byron would ask to be introduced to them. But he always declined this honor—whether out of pride or timidity, or rather a dandy's desire to do exactly the contrary of what others expected. He preferred to spend the evening discussing poetry and philosophy. I remember that we often became so vehement in our arguments that the people in the orchestra would insist we quiet down.

One evening at the height of a philosophical discussion on the principle of utility, M. Silvio Pellico, a charming poet who has since died in an Austrian prison, came and notified Byron that M. Polidori, his physician, had been arrested.

We went in haste to the guard room. M. Polidori, who was tall and very handsome, had been sitting in the orchestra and had been offended by the grenadier's cap of the officer of the guard, which he said prevented him from seeing the singer. He had asked the officer to remove it. (The fact is that despite his Italian name, M. Polidori had been born in England, and consequently he often needed to "vent his spleen on somebody"—to let his ill-humor explode at the expense of something or somebody else.)

Monti, the great poet, had come down to the guard room of La Scala with us. There were fifteen or twenty of us gathered around the prisoner. Everybody was talking at once. M. Polidori was beside himself and red as a beet. Lord Byron, who on the contrary was very pale, was having great difficulty containing his rage. His patrician heart was lacerated to see how little authority or respect he was accorded. At that moment he probably had regrets that he was not an ultra-royalist and hence admitted to the dinners and intimacy of the Archduke Viceroy of Milan. Such was our opinion at any rate.

Whatever the case, the Austrian officer may have thought we formed a nucleus of sedition. If he was scholarly, perhaps memories of the 1740 uprising in Genoa were running through his head. What actually happened is that Monti saw him running out of the guard room to call his soldiers, who took up the rifles they had left outside the door. Then Monti had an excellent idea. He said, *"Sortiamo tutti; restino sola-mente i titolati."* That is, "Let all of us go back to the con-cert hall except those who have titles. Let them stay in the guard room."

Monsignore de Brême remained, along with the Marchese di Sarterana, his brother, Count Confalonieri, and Lord Byron. These gentlemen wrote down their names. When he saw their titles, the officer of the guard forgot the insult to his grenadier's cap and released the prisoner. Immediately this officer had shown his magnanimity, we rendered com-plete justice to him. Actually, he was a good-hearted fellow. Without his grenadier's cap (which was some thirty inches in height) the Austrian officer, who was not even five and a half feet tall, made a poor figure beside M. Polidori, who was a handsome man of six feet. Vanity alone would have prevented many an officer of the guard from releasing his prisoner in such a case.

That same night, at midnight, M. Polidori received an order to leave Milan within twenty-four hours. He was furious and swore that some day he would return and publicly slap the governor who had expelled him. But he never delivered the slap. And two years later he poisoned himself with a whole bottle of prussic acid. (At any rate, *sic dicitur.*)

The day after M. Polidori's departure, Lord Byron, with whom I found myself alone in the immense, empty foyer of La Scala, was complaining in all seriousness that he was being persecuted. "At Copet," he exclaimed through clenched teeth, as if talking to himself and all in a rage, "whenever I entered a salon through one door, all the silly women from

England and Geneva would leave through the other." The last words were not pronounced distinctly enough. Out of consideration for what was either grief or madness, his interlocutor withdrew a few paces. When he came closer again, Byron complained once more, but this time in more modest and general terms. His interlocutor was so unfamiliar with *"i titolati,"* to use Manti's phrase, that he said naïvely to his lordship: "Get your hands on four or five thousand francs, and then start a rumor of your own death. Two or three faithful friends will bury a log in some remote place—the island of Elba, for example. The official report of your death will reach England. Meantime, under the name of Smith or Jones, you will be living in Lima, tranquil and happy. In fact, there is no reason why Mr. Smith, when his hair has turned white, should not come back to live in Europe; or why he should not purchase at a bookstore in Paris or Rome, a copy of the thirtieth edition of *Childe Harold* or *Lara.* And when death really comes to Mr. Smith, he can, if he wants to, enjoy a brilliant and extraordinary moment. He will say: 'The Lord Byron who has been reported dead for thirty years is myself. English society seemed to me so completely stupid that I gave it the slip.' "

Lord Byron answered me coldly: "My cousin, who is to inherit my title, would owe you a fine letter of thanks."

His interlocutor, who had perhaps been indiscreet, stifled a stinging rejoinder.

Byron probably suffered from that unhappy state one often finds in people who have been treated as the spoiled children of fortune: he was consumed by two conflicting desires (a great and certain source of misery). Did he not want, at one and the same time, to be accepted in high society as a lord and to be admired as a poet?

But high society never forgives those who write. It may have been different in the days of Corneille; but even the great Corneille was merely a "good old man" in the eyes of the *noble* Dangeau. (See the latter's *Memoirs.*)

That same evening I chanced to praise the Grand Duke of Tuscany, who certainly deserved it. Byron, who was in a mood of loyalty, was very grateful to me for this.

At that time in Milan they were performing *Elena,* by the
aged Mayer, which has a sublime sextet. The audience would
put up with the first two acts, which were mediocre, in order
to hear this sextet. One night when it was being sung even
better than usual, I was astounded by Byron's eyes: I had
never seen anything so handsome. If a woman had seen them
at such a moment, she would have conceived a passion for
him. I vowed never again to offend such a beautiful soul with
any of those precautionary phrases intended to protect one's
national or individual pride.

I noted [in my journal] that on that same evening we happened to discuss a curious sonnet by Tasso in which he revealed that he was a religious skeptic.

> Odi, Filli, che tuona. . . .
> Ma che cura dobbiam che faccia Giove?
> Godiam noi qui, s'egli è turbato in cielo.
> Tema il volgo i suoi tuoni. . . .
> Pèra il mondo, e rovini! e me non cale
> Se non di quel che più piace a diletta;
> Che, se terra sarò, terra ancor fui.

(Listen, Phyllis, to the thunder. . . . But what should we
care what Jove does? Let us enjoy ourselves here, if he
is disturbed in Heaven. Let the vulgar crowd fear his
thundering! . . . Let the world perish and fall into ruins!
I don't care, except for what pleases and delights me. If I
am to become earth again, well, I was earth before.)

"Those verses are a fit of bad temper and nothing more,"
Byron said. "Tasso's tender soul and wild imagination both
needed to lean on the idea of God. He had too much Platon-
ism cluttering up his mind to be able to put two or three
difficult arguments together. When he wrote that sonnet,
Tasso was feeling his genius; and perhaps he was looking for
both food and a mistress."

With these words, Byron knocked at the door of his inn,
and to our great regret we had to leave him. We were under
his spell—even the wary Italians were. Byron's inn was a
half-league from La Scala, on the edge of a deserted part of

the city. There were a great many thieves; and one had to go through some very sinister narrow streets, alone, at two o'clock in the morning.

All this lent a certain poetic charm to his lordship's retreat. But I cannot understand why he was never attacked. I am sure he would have been very humiliated if he had been relieved of his possessions—because the thieves played some very amusing little tricks on people walking the streets. If it was cold and you were walking along all wrapped up in your overcoat, the thief would toss a barrel hoop over your head, bring it down to arm level, and then rob you at his leisure.

M. Polidori told us that Byron would often write a hundred lines during the morning. At night, upon returning from the opera, excited by the talk or the music, he would take up his manuscript again. Working sometimes until daybreak, he would reduce the hundred lines to twenty or thirty. As soon as he had four hundred or five hundred of them, he would send them off to Mr. Murray, his bookseller in London. When he worked at night he drank a kind of grog consisting of gin and water. But this is another vice he exaggerated in his self-accusation: he was not an immoderate drinker. Often, in order not to gain weight, he would miss a dinner or eat only a plate of vegetables and a little bread. Such a dinner cost only one or two francs. In these cases, using this semblance of a vice as a pretext, Byron would boast of being a miser.

M. Polidori had given us many details on Byron's marriage. The young heiress he married had all of the vanity, and much of the stupidity, of an only daughter. She expected to live the brilliant life of a very great lady. But all she found was a man of genius who wanted neither to command in his own home, nor to be commanded. Lady Byron became irritated. And a malicious servant girl, frightened by Byron's oddities of behavior, aggravated the anger of the mistress of the house. She left her husband. High society grasped a favorable opportunity to *excommunicate* that great man, and his life was poisoned forever.

It was perhaps because of this state of anger and constant unhappiness that he was so sensitive to music, which eased his sorrows and made him shed tears. Byron was sensitive to beautiful music, but with the sensitivity of a new listener. If he had listened to new operas for a year or two, he would have been wild about compositions which, in 1816, gave him no pleasure, and that he even criticized as insignificant or distorted.

I have just learned that Lady Byron (or some priest in her name) is going to reply to Mr. Moore's book. So much the better! If there is discord among the burners of original memoirs, we shall soon see what kind of people Lord Byron fell among.

One day, when we went to visit the echo [site] of La Simonetta, which repeats a pistol shot thirty or forty times and which has been made famous by the *Encyclopedia*, Byron was as delightful as a child, full of gaiety and whimsicality. But the next day, when he arrived at a large ceremonial dinner being given in his honor by Monsignore de Brême, he was as sombre as Talma playing Nero in *Britannicus*. He was the last to arrive; and he had to walk across an immense salon with his slightly twisted foot, while everyone watched him. Far from being indifferent and *blasé*, as he should have been in his role of a dandy, Byron was constantly agitated by some passion. At those moments when the more noble passions were quiescent, he would be tormented by an insane vanity, which took umbrage at everything. But yet if his genius awoke, all was forgotten, the poet was in the heavens, and he took us along with him. What a divine poem he recited for us, one night, on the life of Castruccio Castracani, the Napoleon of the Middle Ages! (We had taken him to see the white marble spires of the Milan Cathedral by moonlight.)

He had one of those weaknesses common among literary men: an extreme sensitivity to praise or blame, especially on the part of other writers. He did not realize that all these judgments are dictated by affectation and that the best of them can only be a *certificat de ressemblance*.

My Italian friends, who were inexorable toward Byron, had noticed that he was proud as a child of the number of languages he could speak. A scholar in Greek—a genuine one, and not a charlatan—who sometimes came to M. de

Brême's box, told us that Byron had a very faulty knowledge of both ancient and modern Greek. The same was true as regards history, despite his claims in this respect.

I almost neglected to mention the astonishing effect produced on Lord Byron by a certain painting by Daniele Crespi. It showed a canon in his bier in the middle of a church who, while the others around him were singing the office of the dead, rises up and cries out: *Justo judicio damnatus sum!* ("I am damned, and God's judgment is just!")

We could not tear Byron away from this painting, which we saw had moved him to horror. Out of respect for his genius we remounted our horses in silence and rode off to wait for him about a mile from the Charterhouse of Castellazo, where Crespi painted frescoes depicting the life of Saint Bruno.[5]

Byron laughed at us the first time we told him there were ten Italian languages instead of one; that, for example, there were two great living poets, Tomaso Grossi and Carline Porta, who wrote in Milanese; and moreover that there was an excellent Italian-Milanese dictionary; and that out of nineteen million Italians, only those living in Rome, Siena, or Florence spoke the language more or less as it was written. Silvio Pellico, the charming poet, said to Byron one day: "Of all these ten or twelve Italian languages whose existence is unknown beyond the Alps, the most beautiful is Venetian. The Venetians are the French of Italy."

"Then they have a living comic poet?"

"Yes," Pellico replied, "and he is excellent. But since he cannot have his comedies performed, he writes them in the form of satires. This charming poet is named Buratti; and every six months the governor of Venice sends him to prison."

[5] In a letter that Lord Byron did me the honor of writing to me in 1823, in order to defend Sir Walter Scott against the charge of excessive servility, he recalled most of those men—as ill-starred as they were likable—whom we had known in Milan in 1816. I detected a trace of cant in Lord Byron's letter; and in order to avoid saying something unpleasant to a man I loved, esteemed, and respected, I did not answer.

In my opinion, it was this remark by Silvio Pellico that decided Byron's future as a poet. (I suspect that inwardly he had a burning desire to see Paris. But he would have wanted the kind of reception that Hume was given in Paris [1765] by the Société Encyclopédique.) Byron eagerly asked for the name of the bookseller who had available the works of Buratti. Because he was now accustomed to the good-hearted humor of the Milanese, we felt free to laugh at him outright. We told him that if M. Buratti wanted to spend his whole life in prison, there was one sure way of doing it, and that was to publish his work. Moreover, where could he find a printer bold enough? Manuscripts of Buratti—very incomplete ones—were selling for three or four sequins. The next day the charming Contessina N. was kind enough to lend her collection to one of us. Byron, who thought he knew the Italian of Dante and Ariosto, was unable to make anything of these verses at first. We went through several of Goldoni's comedies with him; and finally he made a try at the delicious humor of *Omo, Le Strofe,* etc. We were even so improper as to lend him a copy of the *Baffo* sonnets. What a crime in the eyes of Southey! How unfortunate that he did not learn sooner of this atrocious deed!

I believe that Byron wrote *Beppo* and rose to the level of *Don Juan* only because he had read Buratti and seen what delicious pleasure his verses gave to Venetian society. Venice is a world apart whose existence is not even suspected by the melancholy part of Europe. In Venice, one laughs at sorrows. M. Buratti's verses kindle an intoxication in people's hearts. Never have I seen *black on white,* as the Venetians say, produce such an effect. But at this point I can no longer see, and I must leave off writing.

SIR WALTER SCOTT AND
LA PRINCESSE DE CLEVES

Published in *Le National* (edited by Thiers),
February 19, 1830.

THESE TWO NAMES mark the two extremes in the novel. Should one describe the clothes worn by the characters, the landscape around them, and their facial features? Or is it preferable to depict the passions and other feelings that stir their souls? My reflections will not be well received. There is an immense body of literary men with an interest in heaping praises on Sir Walter Scott and his manner of writing. The doublet and brass [leather?] collar of a medieval serf are easier to describe than the emotions of the human heart. One can imagine a medieval costume, or describe it inaccurately (we have only a half-knowledge of the customs [observed] in Cardinal Richelieu's antechamber, and the costumes worn there); but the reader throws down the book in disgust if the author does badly in describing the human heart; if he ascribes, for example, the ignoble sentiments of a lackey to an illustrious comrade-in-arms of the son of Henri IV. Everyone remembers the story of Voltaire giving a lesson in tragic diction to a young actress. When she recited a lively passage very coldly, Voltaire exclaimed, "But, Mademoiselle, you should be acting as though the very devil were in you! What would you do if a cruel tyrant had just taken your lover away from you?" "Monsieur, I'd find another."

I do not maintain that all those who turn out historical novels think as reasonably as that prudent young lady. But not even the most easily offended of them will accuse me of libel if I claim that it is infinitely less difficult to describe a character's costume in picturesque terms than to say what he feels and to make him speak. And let us not forget another advantage of the school of Sir Walter Scott: it takes at least ten pages to describe the costume and posture of a character, however minor he may be. The movements of the soul, which are so difficult to discern and then so difficult to express accurately, without either exaggeration or timidity, would provide only a few lines at the most. Open at random one of the volumes of *La Princesse de Clèves*, read any ten pages, and then compare them with ten pages from *Ivanhoe* or *Quentin Durward*. The merit of the two last-named works is *historical.* They teach a few little details about history to people who are either ignorant of it or know it only slightly. This *historical merit* gives great pleasure. I do not deny that. But it is the historical merit that will fade the soonest. The century will move toward a more simple and natural style; and it will find Sir Walter Scott's mannered approximations as distasteful as they were charming at first. It might perhaps be well to develop further these rapid glimpses into the future destinies of fashionable novels.

Just consider what a great many people have in interest in maintaining that Sir Walter Scott is a great man. But however many there are, I will not put on the mask of hypocrisy so fashionable in the nineteenth century. I will announce quite frankly my conviction that in ten years the Scotch novelist's reputation will have declined by half. Richardson enjoyed in France a fame equal to Scott's. Diderot used to say, "In exile or in prison, I would ask for only three books: Homer, the Bible, and *Clarissa Harlowe.*" Like Scott, Richardson had a bigger reputation in Paris than in England.

Every work of art is a pretty lie. Anyone who has written knows this very well. There is nothing so ridiculous as the advice offered by society people: *imitate life.* Good Lord! I realize that a writer should imitate life. But to what extent? That's the whole question. Racine and Shakespeare were of equal genius. One of them described Iphigenia at Aulis, at the moment when her father is about to sacrifice her. The other described the young Imogen when her husband, whom she adores, is about to have her stabbed in the mountains near Mittford [Milford] Haven. These two great poets both *imitated* life. But one of them wanted to please country gentlemen who still possessed the rough, stern frankness born of the Wars of the Roses. The other sought the applause of polite courtiers who, following the customs established by Lauzun and the Marquis de Vardes, wanted to please the king and win the approval of the ladies. Thus "imitate life" is a meaningless piece of advice. To what extent must life be disguised in order to please the reader? That is the big question.

I believe I must insist on one puerile detail. If a stenographic record had been made of everything said at Aulis when Iphigenia was killed, it would come to five or six volumes, even if it contained only what was said by the characters Racine chose for his play. His first task was to reduce those six volumes to eighty pages. Not only that, but most of the things said by Agamemnon or Calchas would be quite unintelligible today. Or if we did understand them, they would horrify us.

Thus art is nothing more than a pretty lie; but Sir Walter Scott has been too much of a liar. If he had admitted *more natural traits* into his depiction of the passions, he would give greater pleasure to those lofty souls who, in the long run, decide everything in literature. When his characters are in the grip of a passion they seem *ashamed of themselves*— exactly like Mlle Mars when she is playing the role of a stupid woman. When she comes on stage, that great actress gives the audience a knowing look which seems to say: "Don't you ever believe I'm just a stupid woman. I'm quite as smart as you. I just want you to tell me one thing. In trying to please you and win your applause (the thing I care most about), do I not act the role of a stupid woman very well?"

If a painter had this shortcoming of Sir Walter Scott and Mlle Mars, people would say of him: *his colors lack freshness.*

I will go even further: the more lofty the feelings expressed by the Scotch novelist's characters, the less their confidence and boldness. Here one can discern all the experience of an old judge. This is very much the same man who, having been admitted to the table of George IV when the latter was visiting Scotland, eagerly asked for *the glass* from which the King had just drunk to the health of his people. Sir Walter Scott was given the precious goblet, and he put it into the pocket of his overcoat. But by the time he reached home he had forgotten this great favor: he threw down his coat, the glass broke, and he was reduced to despair. Would the elderly Corneille or that good man, Ducis, have understood his despair? When one hundred and forty-six years have passed, Sir Walter Scott will not be regarded so highly as we now regard Corneille, one hundred and fifty-six years after his death.

Appendix

LAMARTINE'S LETTER TO DE MARESTE

Paris, March 19, 1823

I HAVE READ M. Beyle's work with the greatest pleasure. He has said what we all had on the tip of the tongue; and he has made clear and tangible that which was merely a vague perception on the part of everyone with sound judgment. It is to be hoped that he will expand his ideas and be the first to draw up a kind of code for modern literature. I do not mean that he should lay down principles and co-ordinate rules. According to both himself and us, there are no rules apart from examples of genius. But it is plain that there is a certain instinct that prompts the human spirit to leave the beaten path; and it is important that he reveal to himself the goal toward which he aspires and the path by which he can soonest reach that goal. This is what would be accomplished by such a work.

He has come close to complete accuracy in his remarks on the classicists and the romantics. His only sin is one of omission; but that major omission might very well, I feel, lead to plainly false consequences in the continuation of his work. He has forgotten that the imitation of life has not been the only aim of the arts; that *the beautiful*, above all, has been the principle and end of all creations of the human mind. If he had remembered that fundamental truth, he would never have said that Pigault-Lebrun was a romantic (in the favorable sense of the word) but that he was popular, which is something quite different. He would not have said that we must abandon verse in modern poetry.[1] Verse or rhythm is the ideal beauty in expression, or in the form of expression; and because this is so, to abandon it would mean to retrogress. It must be perfected and made more flexible, but not destroyed. The ear is a part of man, and harmony is one of the secret laws of the human spirit: one cannot neglect them without falling into error.

I would appreciate it, my dear De Mareste, if in thanking M. Beyle for the great pleasure I have had from his insights, as ingenious as they are profound and true, you would con-

[1] I.e., poetry in the broad, classical sense—including drama and "fiction" in general. [Translator's note.]

vey to him this simple observation—which if he accepts it will certainly have a good influence on his future ideas. If he does not accept it, we shall not understand each other completely, because I have faith in the beautiful, and the beautiful is not arbitrary: it is because it is.

I should also be gratified if M. Beyle would explain to those who are hard of hearing that the present century does not claim to be romantic in expression (that is, to write differently from those who have written well in the past) but merely in those ideas that time brings with it, or modifies. He should make a concession: classic in expression, romantic in thought. In my opinion, this is the way to be. And I would ask of him a few other concessions of a more serious nature, all of them deriving from the first idea, about which our feelings differ. I believe that the beautiful occupies a higher place in thought than that which he has assigned to it, and that Plato was closer to it than was Condillac.

But I see I have already said too much. Please ask him to forgive me.

ALMA CLASSICS

ALMA CLASSICS aims to publish mainstream and lesser-known European classics in an innovative and striking way, while employing the highest editorial and production standards. By way of a unique approach the range offers much more, both visually and textually, than readers have come to expect from contemporary classics publishing.

LATEST TITLES PUBLISHED BY ALMA CLASSICS

www.almaclassics.com